T0392778

MILESTONES IN STAGING CONTEMPORARY GENDERS AND SEXUALITIES

This introduction to the staging of genders and sexualities across world theatre sets out a broad view of the subject by featuring plays and performance artists that shifted the conversation in their cultural, social, and historical moments.

Designed for weekly use in theatre studies, dramatic literature, or gender and performance studies courses, these ten milestones highlight women and writers of the global majority, supporting and amplifying voices that are key to the field and some that have typically been overlooked. From Paula Vogel, Split Britches, and Young Jean Lee to Werewere Liking, Mahesh Dattani, Yvette Nolan, and more, the chapters place artists' key works into conversation with one another, structurally offering an intersectional perspective on staging genders and sexualities.

Milestones are a range of accessible textbooks, breaking down the need-to-know moments in the social, cultural, political, and artistic development of foundational subject areas.

Emily A. Rollie (PhD) is an associate professor of Theatre and affiliate faculty in Women's, Gender, and Sexuality Studies at Central Washington University, USA.

Milestones Series

Milestones are a range of accessible textbooks, breaking down the need-to-know moments in the social, cultural, political and artistic development of foundational subject areas. Each book maps out ten key moments in the development of its subject, from the emergence of an academic discipline or the chronology of a period in history, to the evolution of an idea or school of thought.

The *Milestones* books are ideal for undergraduate students, either as degree primers or classroom textbooks. The ten key moments make them an ideal fit for weekly class reading and easily digestible for individual study.

Milestones in Dance History
edited by Dana Tai Soon Burgess

Milestones in Asian American Theatre
edited by Josephine Lee

Milestones in Dance in the USA
edited by Elizabeth McPherson

Milestones in Musical Theatre
edited by Mary Jo Lodge

Milestones in Music Education
edited by Clint Randles

Milestones in Digital Journalism
edited by John Pavlik

Milestones in Staging Contemporary Genders and Sexualities
edited by Emily A. Rollie

For more information about this series, please visit: https://www.routledge.com/Milestones/book-series/MILES

MILESTONES IN STAGING CONTEMPORARY GENDERS AND SEXUALITIES

Edited by Emily A. Rollie

Routledge
Taylor & Francis Group

LONDON AND NEW YORK

Designed cover image: © Lust and Comfort image by Eva Weiss, courtesy of Split Britches; For Colored Girls Who Have Considered Suicide/When the Rainbow is Enuf image by and courtesy of Allen Weeks; Indecent image by and courtesy of Jim Carmody; Dance Like a Man image by Kousik Bhowal, courtesy of Barkha Kishnani and ICS Theatre

First published 2024
by Routledge
4 Park Square, Milton Park, Abingdon, Oxon OX14 4RN

and by Routledge
605 Third Avenue, New York, NY 10158

Routledge is an imprint of the Taylor & Francis Group, an informa business

© 2024 selection and editorial matter, Emily A. Rollie; individual chapters, the contributors

British Library Cataloguing-in-Publication Data
A catalogue record for this book is available from the British Library

Library of Congress Cataloging-in-Publication Data
Names: Rollie, Emily A., editor.
Title: Milestones in staging contemporary genders and sexualities / edited by Emily A. Rollie.
Description: London; New York: Routledge, 2024. |
Series: Milestones | Includes bibliographical references and index. | Identifiers: LCCN 2023052054 (print) | LCCN 2023052055 (ebook) | ISBN 9781032225159 (hardback) | ISBN 9781032225135 (paperback) | ISBN 9781003272854 (ebook)
Subjects: LCSH: Sex role in literature. | Sex role in the theater. | Drama—20th century—History and criticism. | Drama—21st century—History and criticism.
Classification: LCC PN56.S52 M55 2024 (print) |
LCC PN56.S52 (ebook) | DDC 809.93353—dc23/eng/20240108
LC record available at https://lccn.loc.gov/2023052054
LC ebook record available at https://lccn.loc.gov/2023052055

ISBN: 9781032225159 (hbk)
ISBN: 9781032225135 (pbk)
ISBN: 9781003272854 (ebk)

DOI: 10.4324/9781003272854

Typeset in Sabon
by codeMantra

To the students, who helped shape this book and will be the future milestone-makers and points in the constellation of art and knowledge.

Contents

Contributors

Heather Jeanne Denyer is Assistant Professor at California State University, Fullerton, where she teaches world theatres, dramaturgy, and puppetry. She has contributed to the following volumes *African Women in Digital Spaces: Redefining Social Movements on the Continent and in the Diaspora*; *The Routledge Companion to Theatre and Politics*; *Puppet and Spirit*, volumes 1 and 2, and *Women and Puppetry: Critical and Historical Investigations*. Her work has received honors, including for her translation of Aristide Tarnagda's play, *Musika* (PAJ 123), and her article on the repatriation of African objects from European museums (*Puppetry International* 49). Look for her co-edited volume of translated plays by Aristide Tarnagda (Bloomsbury) and her website: africantheatresintranslation.org.

Ramón Esquivel is a playwright, director, dramaturg, and educator. He has been an invited playwright at the New Harmony Playwrights Conference, Seven Devils Playwrights Conference, and a winner of the Aurand Harris Memorial Playwriting Award from New England Theatre Conference. Four of his plays are available through Dramatic Publishing: *Luna*; *Nasty*; *Nocturnal*; and *The Hero Twins: Blood Race*. He contributed to *Embodied Playwriting: Improv and Acting Exercises for Writing and Devising*, ed. Hillary Haft Bucs and Clarissa Menafee (Routledge, 2023). Currently Assistant Professor of Theatre at California Polytechnic State University, San Luis Obispo, Ramón teaches courses in playwriting, directing, script analysis, and Latinx Theatre.

Benjamin Gillespie (PhD) is a Doctoral Lecturer in Communication and Gender Studies at Baruch College, City University of New York. His research centers on the intersection of gender, sexuality, and aging in contemporary theatre and drama. Benjamin is co-editor of the *Journal of American Drama and Theatre*. His articles and reviews have been published in *Theatre Journal, Modern Drama, Theatre Survey, Theatre Topics, Performance Research*, and *PAJ* among other journals and scholarly anthologies. Currently, he is editing a new critical anthology on the recent performance work of Split Britches and co-editing the volume *Late Stage: Theatrical Perspectives on Age and Aging*.

Martine Kei Green-Rogers, PhD, is the dean of the Theatre School at DePaul University and a freelance dramaturg. She obtained her BA in Theatre from Virginia Wesleyan College (now Virginia Wesleyan University), her MA in Theatre History and Criticism from The Catholic University of American, and her PhD in Theatre from the University of Wisconsin-Madison. Her publications include articles in the *Routledge Companion to Dramaturgy* and *Theatre History Studies,* and she is co-editor of *Contemporary Black Theatre and Performance Acts of Rebellion, Activism, and Solidarity.*

Marina Johnson (she/they) is a PhD candidate in Theatre and Performance Studies Department at Stanford University. Marina received her MFA in Directing from the University of Iowa. She is the co-host of *Kunafa and Shay*, a podcast produced by HowlRound Theatre Commons. Johnson is a member of Silk Road Rising's Polycultural Institute. Prior to beginning her PhD, she was a Visiting Assistant Professor at Beloit College for three years. For further information, see Marina-Johnson.com

Nabra Nelson is an independent scholar, EDI practitioner and theatre artist from Egypt, Nubia, and California. She is a founding company member of the Seattle-based MENA theatre company, Dunya Productions, a founding company member of the Milwaukee-based womxn-of-color performance troupe Heard Space Arts Collective, leads the Nubian Foundation for Preserving a Cultural Heritage, and is the co-host of the *Kunafa & Shay Theater Podcast* (produced by HowlRound Theatre Commons).

Yvette Nolan (Algonquin) is a playwright, director and dramaturg who works across Turtle Island. Her works include the play *The*

Unplugging, the dance-opera *Bearing*, the libretto *Shanawdithit*, the short play-for-film *Katharsis*, and the VR piece *Reconciling*. She co-created, with Joel Bernbaum and Lancelot Knight, the verbatim play *Reasonable Doubt*, about relations between Indigenous and non-Indigenous communities in Saskatchewan. From 2003 to 2011, she served as Artistic Director of Native Earth Performing Arts, Canada's oldest professional Indigenous theatre. Her book, *Medicine Shows*, about Indigenous performance in Canada was published by Playwrights Canada Press in 2015, and *Performing Indigeneity*, co-edited with Ric Knowles, in 2016.

Emily A. Rollie (PhD, she/her) is a director, intimacy choreographer, and associate professor of theatre at Central Washington University. As a director and intimacy choreographer, Emily has worked in venues around the USA, with emphasis on new play development and intersectional feminist and queer performance. She is associate faculty for Theatrical Intimacy Education (TIE), a founding member of the PNW Theatrical Intimacy Collective, a member of the SDC (Stage Directors and Choreographers Society), and a registered yoga instructor who leads Yoga for Artists workshops. Her research focuses on consent-based performance processes, directing pedagogy and practice, gender studies and feminist/queer theatre.

Bess Rowen (PhD, she/her) is a theatre theorist, historian, and practitioner. Her work focuses on what she terms "affective stage directions," which are stage directions written in ways that engage the physical and emotional responses of future theatre-makers. Her first book, *The Lines Between the Lines: How Stage Directions Affect Embodiment*, was published by University of Michigan Press in 2021. Her next book project focuses on representations of teenage girls on stage. She currently works as an Intimacy Choreographer and continues her training with Theatrical Intimacy Education. Recent articles can be found in *Text & Presentation 2021*, *Modern Drama*, and *Theatre Topics*.

Jashodhara Sen (she/her) is a performance historian and practitioner specializing in South Asian theatre and performance. With an interdisciplinary approach to theatre, her performance practice, scholarship, and teaching are informed by the theories of postcolonialism, decoloniality, and subaltern studies. Her current research, which she is developing in her book project (under contract), *Intersectionality in 'Folk' Performance through Identity and Expression*, focuses on the culturally specific performance form jatra and its many modalities and is centered on class and gender dynamics. The book traces the genealogies of the performance form and highlights jatra's evolution through the interface of a class and gender politics. Her research and reviews have appeared in the *Journal of Dramatic Theory and Criticism*, *Ecumenica*, *Asian Theatre Journal*, *New England Theatre Journal*, *Texas Theatre Journal*, and *Political Theology Network*.

Nicolas Shannon Savard (PhD, they/them) is a queer-trans multidisciplinary artist-scholar, educator, and host of *Gender Euphoria, the Podcast*, a series produced for HowlRound Theatre Commons. Since 2018, they have been touring their autobiographical solo shows, *Five and a Half Feet of Fearsome* and *Un/Packing: A choose-your-own gender adventure*, on the US fringe festival circuit. Their writings on solo and collaborative devised performance, disability aesthetics, and LGBTQ-inclusive pedagogies have been published in the *Journal of Consent-Based Performance*, *Theatre Topics*, and *Texas Theatre Journal*. Savard adapted their dissertation research on US transgender performance histories into an open-access, multimodal, digital archival exhibit entitled *The Queer-Trans Performance Family Tree Project*, which can be found at qtfamilytree.org.

Ngozi Udengwu is a Senior Lecturer in the Department of Theatre and Film Studies of the University of Nigeria, Nsukka, and currently a Fulbright Scholar in Residence at Albany State University, Georgia, USA. She is the author of *Contemporary Nigerian Female Playwrights: A Study in Ideology and Themes*, and more than 40 journal articles and book chapters. A Fellow of the American Council of Learned Societies, Udengwu is currently working on publishing a book based on her postdoc research on Women in the Yoruba Popular Travelling Theatre of Nigeria.

Rachel M.E. Wolfe is a theatre historian with specialties in adaptation and translation theory, theatre history, classics, and feminist theory. Her work, focusing on the intersections of adaptation and gender norms across significant differences in time and culture, has appeared in *Ecumenica: Performance and Religion*, *Journal of Adaptation in Film and Performance*, *Women's Studies: An Interdisciplinary Journal*, and the edited volumes *Vying for the Iron Throne: Essays on Power, Gender, Death and Performance in HBO's Game of Thrones* from McFarland Press and *Troubling Traditions: Canonicity, Theatre, and Performance in the US* from Routledge. Dr. Wolfe is an Associate Professor of Theatre at Utica University in Utica, New York.

Acknowledgments

Special thanks to Eva Weiss and Split Britches, Allen Weeks, Barkha Kishnani and ICS Theatre, and Jim Carmody for their beautiful cover images.

Introduction

Emily A. Rollie

Each time I teach my "Staging Genders" class, I tell my students: "There are a million different ways we could tell the story and arrange the materials of this class." While perhaps hyperbole, the sentiment is true. There are many different ways one might consider and look at milestones in staging genders and sexualities in modern and contemporary performance.

In fact, in 1929, Virginia Woolf wryly lamented in *A Room of One's Own*—a touchstone in feminist literature and gender theory—it is challenging and perhaps impossible to encompass *all* considerations of gender in a single lecture or, in our case, book. Woolf concluded that the "most interesting" way for her to examine gender and literature was to realize that identity, experience, and the works themselves are all "inextricably mixed together" (3). However, as she reminds us, even that has a "fatal drawback": we can never come to a single conclusion because of the myriad ways gender is woven into and expressed by creators and their artistic works.

Of course, this book's title also includes "sexualities," and we recognize that gender and sexuality are two different things. While connected, gender, sex, and sexuality are, in fact, often misunderstood terms. In casual conversation, sometimes the terms are mistakenly used interchangeably—particularly "gender" and "sex."

Following the work of gender theorists like Judith Butler, **gender** is socially constructed, meaning that social norms, expectations, and structures inform understanding of gender. Butler also argues that gender is performative: "Gender is in no way a stable identity or locus of agency from which various acts proceed; rather, it is an identity tenuously constituted in time—an identity, instituted through a stylized repetition of acts" (519).

DOI: 10.4324/9781003272854-1

There is an important difference here between gender as *performative* and gender as *performed*. One cannot simply choose to perform gender, taking it on and off like a simple costume. Instead, gender is performative, meaning that it is seen and understood as a repetition of something that came before and is socially constructed and informed, meaning that the world around us also plays a key part in shaping our ideas about and performances of gender.

Because gender is socially constructed, it follows that our understandings of gender are informed through different cultural assumptions, interpretations, and contexts and over time. Often, gender has been constructed to be viewed as a strict binary (man/woman, male/female), but current understandings remind us that gender, **gender identity**, and **gender expression** are expansive, dynamic, and on a spectrum.

Sex and **sex assigned at birth** refer to biological, hormonal, genetic composition, and sex is often assigned at birth as male or female. However, researchers like Anne Fausto Sterling have pointed out that many people are born with no clear singular sex, so more frequently, the term "sex assigned at birth" refers to the idea that the sex assignment often happens without the agency of the person. The term **"cisgender"** refers to individuals whose gender identity aligns with their birth-assigned sex.

And then there's **sexuality.** Sometimes called sexual orientation, this is a person's sexual feelings, thoughts, desires, identities, and values, and includes sexual identity and sometimes romantic identity. An individual's sexual orientation and identity are independent of their gender identity.

While genders and sexualities are distinctly different, we also see the ways that they often are addressed and considered in conversation with each other, and in conversation with other intersectional identities such as race, ability, ethnicity, body diversity, and more. To get at the complex relationship between them and how that often emerges in performance, this text grounds itself in **intersectionality**—a term coined by Kimberlé Crenshaw to speak to the multiple social forces, social identities, and ideological systems through which power and disadvantage are expressed and legitimized—as we explore milestones in staging genders and sexualities.

"WAIT … WHAT *IS* A MILESTONE?"

In this book, we are interested in troubling the rigidity of a single linear chronology. Very often that approach implies that there is only *one* history and that events happen only in a cause-and-effect manner—all of which is often a mode of thinking supported by white, patriarchal, **heteronormative** structures.

Particularly in queer and feminist considerations of histories, there is a need to "highlight the intergenerational linkages" between queer and feminist artists and draw from a "non-linear clustering of works that would highlight influences and legacies" as well as would "challenge the implications of straight time and heteronormative life course models" (Gillespie and Rowen 69).

Rather than the linear, this-happened-and-then-this-happened approach, we recognize that milestones can happen simultaneously and may have larger echoes and longer impacts. As such, this volume considers our "milestones" as touchstones in a larger constellation of artistic work. All of the works and artists featured here are linked to and in conversation with each other—some more directly than others. Together, their voices and works offer a way of looking at historical and contemporary theatrical works together as well as the relationships between artists, over time, and across geographical borders.

In fact, just days before I finished this introduction in October 2023, The Kilroys—a collective of US theatre artists who has, beginning in 2014, published The Kilroy's List which recommends new works by trans, nonbinary, and women playwrights each year—reimagined their annual list. As articulated on their website, they are "shaking shit up," transforming their list to The Web to show the connections and relationships between artists and works rather than emphasize a ranked list or hierarchy.

Whether a web or a constellation, we aim in this volume to push back against singular, hierarchical narratives and instead seek connections, resonances, and relationships between the artists and works. And ideally, we hope that thinking about these artists and works as part of a constellation or web of works will launch you into finding and making connections of your own.

"SO WHAT DOES THAT *MEAN?*"

It means you may see some gaps in time as well as some clusters of pieces and artists emerging in similar moments of time. It means that you may see some works or artists that are considered more "canonical" and "well known" alongside others that are less widely known. But all offer key interventions and expansions in the conversation around staging genders and sexualities. It means each chapter focuses on two or more representative pieces (so you can dig into specific touchstones and explore concrete examples), while also referencing other works and artists that are connected to the representative pieces.

It also means that, as editor, I had to make some difficult choices, leaving out some artists and works that I love and regularly teach.[1] Thus, I recognize (and mourn) the gaps that some might point to here. For instance, Caryl Churchill, a common name in courses like Staging Genders, Women and Performance, or Feminist Performance, doesn't have a specific chapter. However, her work certainly intersects with and is contemporary to many of those included.

Churchill emerged in the UK during the early 1970s, a time when most British stages were dominated by male voices and theatre-makers. Despite this, she created innovative, experimental work that pushed the boundaries of not only whose stories were told on stage, but also how those stories were being staged—similar to the artists you will read about throughout the rest of this book. She has a keen political sensibility and interest in both exploding linear structure and undertaking collaborative research and creation, as evidenced by the plays she wrote as part of the Joint Stock collective theatre company in the United Kingdom during the 1970s.

Of those productions, *Cloud 9* (1979) is commonly referenced and taught for its theatrical examination of gender, race, and histories. As argued by many early and foundational feminist critics such as Sue-Ellen Case, Gayle Austin, Kate Davy, and others, the genre of realism presents a challenge for feminist, queer, and BIPOC creators. As Jill Dolan writes:

> Feminist performance theory argued that ideology is inevitably written into form, and that realism—with its resolutely domestic locales, its box sets, its middle-class, bourgeois proprieties, and its conservative moralizing against outsiders who threaten the normative social order—was bound to marginalize and demonize women and others who don't fit conventional models of white, male, middle-class, heterosexual decorum. (437)

Further, in their published dialogue "Dream While You Read: A Map for Venturing Beyond Theatrical Realism," Danilo Gambini and Roger Q. Mason argue for the need to "expand your imagination beyond all kinds of binaries … And it's because of that expansiveness that we can imagine freedoms on the page. The world is too confined in their [white, cisgender, patriarchal] realism."

As such, many feminist, queer, global majority theatre-makers intentionally push back against realism and its position within **whiteness** and **patriarchy**, a strategy seen across the work of many of the artists included in these chapters.

Of course, while many push away from realism, still others like Beth Henley (*Crimes of the Heart*), Lynn Nottage (*Ruined*), Dominique Morisseau *(Pipeline, Detroit '67)*, and others in this volume also create within it, consciously deploying realism as a way to re-write it from within to center gender alongside race, sexuality, class, ability, and other intersectional identities.

In many works featured in the following pages, artists also examine existing narratives and histories, re-framing them to illuminate issues related to gender. Churchill's *Cloud 9*, for instance, brings together genres of melodrama, operetta, and realism to explore gender over time and histories as well as its intersections with race. It traces the impacts and legacies of sexism, colonization, and racism, with Act I set in colonial Africa and Act II occurring 25 years later focusing on the children of Act I. Within this structure, Churchill also deems it "essential" that specific roles are played across gender and race as a way to raise questions about and complicate the socially created ideas of gender, race, and sexuality. Similarly and in conversation with Churchill, many of the artists and works included here probe the complicated facets of gender and sexuality within larger structures of patriarchy, heteronormativity, **white supremacy**, and capitalism.

Because the power structures of the patriarchy and white supremacy often privilege white men's voices and works, we intentionally feature milestone works in this volume that are written and created by theatre-makers who are women, trans, nonbinary, and/or of the global majority, and the essays are written by contributors who hail from a variety of professional and scholarly backgrounds—playwrights, dramaturgs, directors, performers, scholars, teachers—with several co-written essays to promote further conversations and the sharing of knowledge.

As you read, you may notice that artists and collaborators are referenced across chapters—such as the connection between Spiderwoman Theatre of New York and the Canadian Indigenous theatre company Native Earth Performing Arts. We hope that you use these connections as your own sort of scavenger hunt and that you continue to locate more and more points on the intersecting constellation of staging genders and sexualities both in the book and beyond.[2]

FURTHER RESOURCES

French, Sarah. *Staging Queer Feminisms: Sexuality and Gender in Australian Performance, 2005–2015*. Palgrave Macmillan, 2017.

This scholarly text considers sexuality and gender in 21st-century Australian performance and the ways it expands on earlier explorations of gender that occurred during the 1980s and 1990s.

Werth, Brenda and Katherine Zien, eds. *Bodies on the Front Lines: Performance, Gender, and Sexuality in Latin America and the Caribbean*. University of Michigan Press, 2024.

This edited volume considers gender in Latin America and Caribbean performances with an emphasis on activism and the ways performance informs protests.

Wolf, Stacy. *A Problem Like Maria: Gender and Sexuality in the American Musical*. University of Michigan Press, 2002.

A foundational name in feminist musical theatre, Wolf's text offers a clear starting point for considerations of gender and sexuality in US musical theatre.

REFERENCES

Butler, Judith. "Performative Acts and Gender Constitution: An Essay in Phenomenology and Feminist Theory." *Theatre Journal*, vol. 40, no. 4, 1988, pp. 519–531.

Dolan, Jill. "Feminist Performance Criticism and the Popular: Reviewing Wendy Wasserstein." *Theatre Journal*, vol. 60, 2008, pp. 433–457.

Gambini, Danilo, and Roger Q. Mason. "Dream While You Read: A Map for Venturing Beyond Theatrical Realism." *American Theatre*, July 21, 2022. https://www.americantheatre.org/2022/07/21/dream-while-you-read-a-map-for-traveling-beyond-theatrical-realism/. Accessed January 3, 2024.

Gillespie, Benjamin, and Bess Rowen. "Against Chronology: Intergenerational Pedagogical Approaches to Queer Theatre and Performance Histories." *Theatre Topics*, vol. 30, no. 2, July 2020, pp. 69–83.

The Kilroys. *The Kilroys 2023 Web*. October 14, 2023. https://thekilroys.org/web-2023/. Accessed January 3, 2024.

Woolf, Virginia. *A Room of One's Own*. 1929. E-book ed., Global Grey, October 15, 2012. https://www.globalgreyebooks.com/room-of-ones-own-ebook.html. Accessed January 3, 2024.

NOTES

1 Just a few include Leilah Assunção, Jocelyn Bioh, Carmen Boullosa, Lauren Gunderson, Taylor Mac, Josefina Lopez, Charles Ludlam, Susana Torres Molin, Suzan-Lori Parks, Winsome Pinnock, Djanet Sears, Erin Shields, Tim Miller, Azure D. Osborne-Lee, and Mary Kathryn Nagle.
2 We are interested in hearing about your additional constellation points and connections. As you engage with this text and build your constellations, please update us via email (StagingGendersBook@gmail.com).

CHAPTER 1

The Enduring Legacy of Ntozake Shange and Adrienne Kennedy

Martine Kei Green-Rogers

Black Feminism and the works of Black women artists have long gone hand-in-hand. The canonical early dramatic literature texts written by Black women dealt with the intersections of race, gender, class, and identity. The first known anti-lynching play, *Rachel*, by Angelina Weld Grimke, was published in 1916. This play opened a new period in African American dramatic history because it was "the first non-musical for which we have an extant script that was written by an African American woman and publicly performed by black actors" (Stephens 332). *Rachel*'s critical appeal lay in its compelling argument to all women, regardless of race, about the importance of motherhood. As Stephens writes: "Grimke was attempting to make white women question the desirability of motherhood from an African-American woman's perspective at a time when lynchings were at an all-time high" (334). Grimke's use of the mostly universal female reality of motherhood to illustrate how lynchings affect African American women bridged a gap that allowed for a connection between white and African American women on a different level than just solidarity as women—now as women with families.

The same is true of queer feminist Mary P. Burrill's plays *They That Sit in Darkness* (1919) and *Aftermath* (1919). Similar to Grimke's *Rachel*, Burrill's *They That Sit in Darkness* considers the impact and cyclical nature of poverty on Black families, particularly Black woman. When the family's matriarch dies shortly after childbirth, her teenaged daughter Lindy, the eldest of seven, must give up her dreams of an education at Tuskegee Institute to take care of her younger siblings. Through the play, Burrill powerfully pushes back against racialized stereotypes and portrayals of the time, arguing that Black poverty did not come from inferiority or laziness but the "cyclical oppression which trapped African Americans and, in particular, black women"—an examination that also brought conversations about birth control and reproductive rights to the stage (Smith 3).

Burrill's *Aftermath* also is in conversation with Grimke's *Rachel* but brings in considerations of masculinity and Black manhood. *Aftermath* centers on John, a young soldier fighting in World War I. When he returns home from the war, John finds out that his father has been the victim of a lynching. Facing the fact that his service in the military does not guarantee his or any other Black person's rights, John seeks revenge on the white man responsible for the murder of his father. The play asked provocative questions about the ways that Black soldiers fought for their community abroad but they and their families faced oppression and violence at home. *Aftermath* boldly confronted systemic racism and sexism, offering Black women a means of artistic social activism through the arts previously unheard of due to literary, gender, and socioeconomic barriers. Burrill's work became one of the first in this type of play to directly point a finger at the systematic means of oppression that plagued the country in the early 1900s and constantly made Black peoplehood during this period difficult.

Grimke and Burrill, along with others whom we know of and still others who are lost to history, began to pave the way for how Black women playwrights used their art to address what would eventually be known as the Black Feminist movement. Black Feminism, as practiced in the United States, is a type of **feminism** specifically focusing on and foregrounding the experiences of Black women. Of course, Black women are not a monolith, so there are varying ways in which Black Feminism manifests in the work of Black Feminists. However, according to Max Peterson in *The*

Revolutionary Practice of Black Feminisms for the National Museum of African American History and Culture:

> a few foundational principles do exist among black feminisms: Black women's experience of racism, sexism, and classism are inseparable. Their needs and worldviews are distinct from those of black men and white women. There is no contradiction between the struggle against racism, sexism, and all other-isms. All must be addressed simultaneously.

It is with this understanding of the foundational principles of Black Feminism, that we begin to see the traditions of the exploration of Black women's lives laid out by writers such as Burrill and Grimke. From those traditions, we find the pathway to the genius of the works by Ntozake Shange and Adrienne Kennedy in addressing the complex lives of Black women in the United States.

NTOZAKE SHANGE, HER WORK, AND HER BLACK FEMINIST LEGACY[1]

Born Paulette Linda Williams on October 18, 1948, Ntozake Shange ("Ntozake" in the Zulu dialect Xhosa means "she who comes with her own things" and "Shange" means "she who walks like a lion") was a prolific poet, theatre artist, dancer, and educator. Shange's poetry collections include *Nappy Edges* (1978) and *Ridin' the Moon in Texas* (1987). She also published the novels *Sassafrass, Cypress & Indigo* (1982), about the lives of three sisters; the semi-autobiographical *Betsey Brown* (1985); and *Liliane* (1994), a coming-of-age story about a wealthy Black woman. In addition, Shange wrote several children's books, including *Whitewash* (1997). One constant thread within her writings is the intersection of where Black women's lives, racism, sexism, and the world around them collide. As Neal A. Lester states, "Shange champions the woman of color specifically and people of color generally as they move toward optimal self-consciousness, positive self-identity, and unlimited self-realization in an oppressive and blatantly sexist and racist modern society" (718).

Over the course of her career, Shange won numerous accolades and awards for her work including an Obie award, a Guggenheim Fellowship, and the proclamation of "Ntozake Shange Day" by Congressman Charles Rangel on June 14, 2014, in New York, NY. Shange passed away October 27, 2018, at the age of 70 in Maryland.

In 1975, Shange created the "**choreopoem**," a genre and style of theatre that combines dance, poetry, and music/song to elicit an emotional response from an audience, through her theatrical piece for *colored girls who have considered suicide / when the rainbow is enuf.* The piece, revolutionary for the time, centered arond seven women who are named for the colors they wear and who deliver 20 poems that focus on themes such as sexual violence, domestic abuse, and abandonment as well as the joy, laughter, empowerment, and light that can be found in the everyday lives of women of color. This piece is now a canonical theatrical text as well as a highly visible example of how the Black Feminist movement manifested in the theatre.

In addition to the innovative structure of the choreopoem, the revolutionary aspect of this play was in its representations of Black women's lives, particularly in comparison to other pieces written by other Black women. There was an oral, aural, and visual difference in the way Shange depicted the "everydayness" of the dialogue of the women characters at the center of the script. These characters say the things that most women know, have seen with their own eyes, have heard with their own ears, and have personal experiences with in a way that is specific to Black culture at the time. Shange made the choice to focus on the less recognized narratives of Black women and acknowledged that she was serving a larger purpose with her writing. She named herself a "cultural war correspondent" and, in many ways, this is where her true Black Feminist writer self shines the brightest (Brown-Guillory 113). If a war correspondent is a person who covers, first-hand, stories from war zones, Shange covered, first-hand, the cultural war zones of racism and sexism in the language of those directly affected by the cultural war.

A moment in the play that embodies the Black Feminist movement and illustrates how Shange became a "cultural war correspondent" comes in the form of focusing a bright spotlight on an experience that transcends race but is also colored (pun intended) by the color of the woman's skin. In an interview with Elizabeth Brown-Guillory, Shange mentions that there is no subject she will avoid. More specifically, she says: "There is violence perpetrated against Black people that needs to be acknowledged," and she saw her work as a place to acknowledge this violence (121). The way society treats survivors of sexual assaults, making a tragic incident appear as though it was the survivor's fault, clearly explains why many women do not come forward when they are assaulted, and Shange is determined to highlight, while also complicating, that narrative specifically from the Black woman's perspective.

In the scene "I'm The Poet Who," the lady in orange speaks about how the language she is interested in is the one created through her body when she dances. Shange provides, through the lady in orange, a very visual and poetic representation of what happens when a woman is aware of her body and how it moves. The freedom and joy of this moment is broken quickly as Shange transitions into a section titled "Latent Rapists":

> lady in blue.
> a friend is hard to press charges against
>
> lady in red.
> if you know him
> you must have wanted it
>
> lady in purple.
> a misunderstanding
>
> lady in red.
> you know
> these things happen
>
> lady in blue.
> are you sure
> you didn't suggest

> lady in purple.
> had you been drinkin
>
> lady in red.
> a rapist is always to be a stranger
> to be legitimate
> someone you never saw
> a man wit obvious problems. (33)

This passage resonates for any person who has been in a situation in which their trauma has been explained away. These characters say the sad truth—that the proximity of knowledge of the survivor to the perpetrator directly correlates to a decrease in the likelihood of justice resulting from the offense.

Shange also proves herself to be firmly planted at the intersection of cultural war correspondent and Black Feminism in her purposeful distortion of the King's/Queen's English, a term used to refer to the so-called "standard" or "correct" speech and usage of English. As The Combahee River Collective, a Black lesbian feminist socialist organization active in Boston, Massachusetts, from 1974 to 1980, declared in their 1977 statement, notably only a few years after Shange's play debuted: "Even our Black women's style of talking/testifying in Black language about what we have experienced has a resonance that is both cultural and political" (973). Shange articulated and embodied this sentiment long before the Combahee River Collective actively addressed it, stating:

> I was taking a creative writing class once and was told by the professor that you can't detour from the King's English unless you do it on purpose. If you don't do it on purpose, then you're not in control of what you're doing and you don't know what the implications are. (Lester 728)

She realized that one of the most powerful things she could do, which is illustrated in the quote from the script, is to manipulate the language of the play to help make her point. Later in that same interview, she says that the point of this purposeful reappropriation of language was to "know your enemy so well that you're able to do something with his weapon"—his language (Lester 728). If the part of the play discussed earlier

Fig. 1.1 The cast of *for colored girls ...* , Penumbra Theatre, Saint Paul, MN, 2018. Photo by Allen Weeks.

is any indicator, Shange distorts the language of that moment (in the cases of "drinkin" and "wit," for instance) for two purposes. One, to capture the dialect of the women she is representing for the purposes of the "cultural and political." But also, to a larger point, to disrupt how language is used to oppress women of color. These purposeful manipulations of the lexicon illustrate how "proper" oppression can be combated by embracing Black culture's "improper" but stylistic grammar. There is power and purpose in telling a story, even the more painful ones, in one's own vernacular.

There are other moments in the play in which Shange continues the work of pointing out how women come to moments of self-discovery about their worth. The lady in yellow states:

> but bein alive & bein a woman & bein colored is a
> metaphysical dilemma
> i havent conquered yet
> do you see the point my spirit is too ancient to
> understand the separation of soul & gender
> my love is too delicate to have thrown back on my face. (61)

Shange, in this moment, uplifts intersectionality, hearkens to the ancestors and the spiritual reality of many Black and Brown women, and makes a discovery of self while crafting a lesson that all women need to hear—that they are worthy. The lady in yellow helps us understand, through the text of the play as well as in performance, how important cultural and personal revelations can be found just underneath the surface of a lyrical stream of consciousness.

The impact of Shange's positionality and artistry within this play can be found in the reviews of the show. The show had a small first run in 1976 at the Anspacher Theatre in New York and was met with critical acclaim. Clive Barnes (and it is important to note here, a white critic) of *The New York Times* wrote on June 2, 1976: "To be black and to be a woman is a kind of double infirmity that must be faced with courage. Miss Shange's evening of prose and poetry ... is a lyric and tragic exploration into black woman's awareness." He continued to say that "Miss Shange writes with such exquisite care and beauty that anyone can relate to her message" and that "fundamentally—if we have any sensitivity or sensibility at all—we all feel the same things. We just need poets and other strangers to point them out to us" (42). The masterful work that Shange did with this play—and the work's acknowledgment by a prominent white critic—illustrates how important Shange's technique and voice was to the Black Feminist movement. She brought mainstream critical attention to the joys and the plights of Black women through her work.

The themes of the play have stood the test of time. Shange and her works stand as a foremother to movements such as MeToo, founded by activist Tarana Burke in 2006, and Black Lives Matter, movements that are meant to empower and highlight the experiences of Black people while also troubling the larger systematic forces that inhibit true equality. As such, Shange's words and stories tend to ring truer (or at least ring as equally as true) now than they may have at the moment in which the play premiered. In a world in which violence against women garners national and international attention, yet those experiences within communities of color are still marginalized, the stories of these women in *for colored girls* channel the energy of all the stories of women who came before the play and, unfortunately, those who are yet to come into a place where community, sharing, and healing may begin.

ADRIENNE KENNEDY, HER WORK, AND ITS BLACK FEMINIST LEGACY

Born September 13, 1931, Adrienne Kennedy is best known for the play *Funnyhouse of a Negro*, which premiered in 1964. Her works also include *The Owl Answers* (1965), *A Rat's Mass* (1967), *The Lennon Play: In His Own Write* (1967), *A Beast's Story* (1969), *Sun: A Play for Malcolm X Inspired by His Murder* (1968), *A Lesson in Dead Language* (1968), *Electra and Orestes* (1972), *The Ohio State Murders* (1992), *Sleep Deprivation Chamber* (1996), and *He Brought Her Heart Back in a Box* (2018).

Much of her work explores issues of race, family, kinship, and violence in American society and tends to be autobiographical. As outlined by Werner Sollors in *The Adrienne Kennedy Reader*, Kennedy draws on the mythical and historical, while also transcending character and plot through ritualistic repetition, poetic alienation, and radical structural experimentation, to depict and explore the African American female experience; Kennedy combines her very personal experiences of these larger systemic issues with the use of surrealism in her plays to create a juxtaposition that results in a visceral audience experience (vii). In 1969, *The New York Times* critic Clive Barnes wrote: "While almost every black playwright in the country is fundamentally concerned with realism ... Miss Kennedy is weaving some kind of dramatic fabric of poetry." Long story short, Kennedy's plays are a heightened artistic, emotional, and intellectual journey that are both poignant and disorienting for an audience.

This is especially true in her most known work, *Funnyhouse of a Negro*, in which the main character, Sarah, explores the historical and cultural violence at war within herself as a result of her mixed race background. Because this piece, and frankly, most of Kennedy's works are encountered predominately in academic classroom settings, this chapter purposefully focuses on a different, more contemporary piece of Kennedy's that has seen larger critical review. This approach will help us situate Kennedy with Shange in a larger and ongoing cultural and societal context of revolutionary Black Feminism in performance.

Kennedy's play, *He Brought Her Heart Back in a Box*, synthesizes interracial relationships, the promise of a Black woman's intellect, the inherent danger of the Jim Crow South in the 1940s, and the potential of the transcendence of that danger in the North—with devastating consequences and legacies. As the rise of Nazism looms in the background of the play, we learn about the love blossoming between Chris (a White man) and Kay (a Black woman). The story of the play mostly unfolds as letters between Chris, writing from his dressing room at a theatre where he is pursuing his career as an actor, and Kay, writing from the Black section of a train car on her way to an Historically Black College, and it finds us initially rooting for the love between them despite all odds that come from life and racial structures of this time period. The play, before the two lovers separate and must communicate through letters, starts in a place that foreshadows the eventual, unfortunate end for these two: a production of Christopher Marlowe's *The Massacre at Paris*. This rarely produced 1593 work discusses a historic betrayal—the slaughter of France's Huguenots by the Catholic monarchy's troops, urged on by the Machiavellian Duke of Guise. We come to find out that a very similar betrayal, complete with a Machiavellian history in the guise (pun intended) of the legacy of a powerful grandfather and replicated through Chris's father, is on the horizon for these lovers.

Kennedy's play, documenting the outrages of a racist past, has a dire ending. Racism persists through human betrayal and destructiveness, and it is not able to be dismantled by the power of human love. Kennedy continues to foreshadow the end of the road for these two lovers beyond the Marlowe reference, bringing to the forefront the lovers' fondness for the romantic songs of Noel Coward's 1930 operetta, *Bitter Sweet*, which also has a doomed love embedded in its story. The tragic story that chases Kay and Chris is anchored in the town of their origin, Montefiore. The town, built by Chris's father and grandfather, is sharply divided between white and Black. But it is also the kind of small Southern US town in which the groups are closely interrelated, and everybody knows everyone. For example, Chris's father, who planned the town's segregated layout, also has personally built and landscaped a cemetery for its nonwhite population, providing burial plots for the mothers of Chris's mixed-race half-siblings. The "separate and not as equal—but still publicly prominent" display of miscegenation, adultery, and outright abuse of Black women's bodies by the progenitor of the town is acutely visible.

On the other side of this story, the promise and potential of a Black woman's life comes into full view. Kay is coming into her own as a person. While she tragically lost her mother, she is figuring out what the legacy of her mother and her mother's untimely death means for her own future. The product of a mixed-race relationship, Kay finds that she has things in common with Chris, but she also does not benefit from her proximity to whiteness in the same way that Chris does. They have very different perspectives on and experiences in the world; Chris is working on his acting career while Kay is on the way to her Historically Black College to begin her studies for the year.

A story of hidden histories, convolution, miscommunication, and deception begins to unfold in numerous ways that affect the two lovers' ability to understand and relate to one another. Separated and now living in different parts of the United States, they learn about each other's past and present through the mouths of others. For example, Kay recounts to Chris knowledge that her maternal grandmother passed on to warn her of the ramifications of continuing to see Chris. We also hear a disorienting story of how Kay's mother was rejected by her wealthy white partner Charles and his family, maltreated by her mother, and ultimately fled to Cincinnati a few days after Kay's birth—only to end up dead shortly thereafter. The story posits the rumor that either Charles tracked Kay's mother down and murdered her or that Kay's mother shot herself.

Communication between the two lovers is further complicated by Chris's father, who is represented by a puppet in the play. The puppet, who watches Kay while she sits in the colored section of the train, becomes an eventual impediment to the two. As such, it becomes very apparent that Kennedy is making a pointed symbolic choice to highlight the ways in which White Supremacist ideology as well the prominence of white male patriarchy as a generational plague continues to manifest. The artistic choice of a puppet to "puppet" information passed down from generation to generation echoes how Kennedy uses surrealism to tackle another larger issue that we see regularly in her work—the internal struggle for mixed-race women.

In the end, Kay and Chris decide to meet in New York and marry, but their dream of settling in Paris after the war remains unfulfilled. Their death at the end of the play feels reminiscent of the tragedy that befell Kay's mother. This ending, like other plays in Kennedy's canon, illustrates that there are some symbolic eventualities that cannot be avoided. As Jennifer Krasinski states: "This play, like so much of Kennedy's writing, takes stock of stories as both birthright and burden, as weight and warning for an unsettled future" (48). In the end, literal and metaphorical blood falls as a result of the racism and sexism that is ingrained in the fabric of the United States and lives in the background of most Black Americans.

Michel Fiengold echoes this ultimate lesson in his review of the play in 2018 stating that Kennedy "refracts all of world history and its attendant cultural artifacts through the prism of the American shame, racism, and the personal agonies it has visited on generations of individuals." This lesson is the one that catapults Kennedy work into an echelon of work rooted in and part of the legacy of Black Feminism.

SHANGE AND KENNEDY'S LEGACY ON BLACK FEMINISM

Shange and Kennedy were writing at a moment in which the narrative of Black women in the theatre tended to be relegated to Christian saints, whores, mothers, or slaves if the narratives were not written by Black women (and, unfortunately, these stereotypes could also be found in much of the work of Black men at the time). The work of these women and others such as J.e. Franklin, Barbara Ann Teer, and more were key to part of the Black Arts Movement, a movement during the 1960s and 1970s that sought to rewrite and amplify the narratives of Black life and advocated for the "nothing for us, without us" ideology that would propel Black American culture into the 1990s.

The work of Shange and Kennedy illustrate the importance of intersectionality in feminism, as it was necessary to truly capture the truth of Black women's experiences in the United States. Their Black Feminist legacy endures in what would become Womanism (a term coined by Alice Walker in the early 1980s and that, while celebrating all women, is culturally informed, placing special focus on issues specific to women of color and Black women) and the Queer Black Feminist movement, and it continues through the work of contemporary (as of the publication of this chapter) Black women artists. Organizations, like the aforementioned Combahee River Collective, took the thoughts brought into the world by artists such as Shange and Kennedy and incorporated them, directly or indirectly, within their Manifesto by asserting that:

> We believe that sexual politics under patriarchy is as pervasive in Black women's lives as are the politics of class and race. We also often find it difficult to separate race from class from sex oppression because in our lives they are most often experienced simultaneously. We know that there is such a thing as racial-sexual oppression which is neither solely racial nor solely sexual, e.g., the history of rape of Black women by white men as a weapon of political repression. (972)

Additionally, contemporary artists such as Suzan-Lori Parks, Stacey Rose, Katori Hall, and numerous others' approaches to discussing the worlds of Black women through their work have threads that can be traced back to the work of these important women who have shaped and continue to inform the legacy of staging genders and Black Feminism.

FURTHER RESOURCES

Forsgren, La Donna. *In Search of Our Warrior Mothers: Women Dramatists of the Black Arts Movement.* Northwestern University Press, 2018.
This book explains the Black Arts Movement and, more specifically, examines the careers of four women within the movement: Martie Evans-Charles, J.e. Franklin, Sonia Sanchez, and Barbara Ann Teer. These women and their work were prominent within the movement while also remaining relatively obscure within a larger mainstream historical conversation about the movement. Forsgen's book brings brighter focus and well-deserved attention to these artists.
Kennedy, Adrienne, and Werner Sollors. *The Adrienne Kennedy Reader.* University of Minnesota Press, 2001.
This collection places the majority of Kennedy's work in one place. An introduction by Werner Sollors also helps contextualize Kennedy's canon and literary development for a larger audience.
Tellini, Silvia Mara. "Experimental Language Deconstructing Patriarchal Discourse in Ntozake Shange's for colored girls who have considered suicide/ when the rainbow is enuf." *American, British, and Canadian Studies,* vol. 25, no. 1, 2015, pp. 155–170. This article delves into the ways Shange uses and deconstructs language to bring attention to patriarchal structures in her play. As such, it helps continue and extend the ideas discussed in this chapter.

REFERENCES

Barnes, Clive. "Black Sisterhood: Ntozake Shange's For Colored Girls Opens at Papp's Anspacher Theater." *The New York Times,* June 2, 1976, p. 42.
Brown-Guillory, Elizabeth. "Ntozake Shange: A Cultural War Correspondent—An Interview." *CLA Journal,* vol. 62, no. 2, 2019, pp. 111–131.

Fiengold, Michael. "Adrienne Kennedy's 'He Brought Her Heart Back in a Box' Spins a Terrifying Tale of Poetry, Racism, and Doomed Love." *The Village Voice,* February 6, 2018. https://www.villagevoice.com/adrienne-kennedys-he-brought-her-heart-back-in-a-box-spins-a-terrifying-tale-of-poetry-racism-and-doomed-love. Accessed December 30, 2023.

Combahee River Collective. "The Combahee River Collective Statement: A Black Feminist Statement." *Encyclopedia of African-American Writing,* 3rd edn., ed. Bryan Conn and Tara Bynum. Grey House Publishing, 2018, pp. 971–976.

Krasinski, Jennifer. "GRACEFULNESS MUST BE SOUGHT." *Artforum International,* vol. 56, no. 8, April 2018, pp. 47–48.

Lester, Neal A. "At the Heart of Shange's Feminism: An Interview." *Black American Literature Forum,* vol. 24, no. 4, 1990, pp. 717–730. JSTOR, https://doi.org/10.2307/3041798.

Peterson, Max. "The Revolutionary Practice of Black Feminisms." National Museum of African American History and Culture, https://nmaahc.si.edu/explore/stories/revolutionary-practice-black-feminisms. Accessed September 24, 2023.

Sollors, Werner and Adrienne Kennedy. *The Adrienne Kennedy Reader.* University of Minnesota Press, 2001.

Shange, Ntozake. *for colored girls who have considered suicide/ when the rainbow is enuf.* Scribner, 1997 (reprint).

Smith, David B. "Intersectionality in the Dramas of Mary Burrill, Alice Childress, and Pearl Cleage." *Continuum: The Journal of the African Diaspora Drama,* vol. 1, no. 2, January 2015, pp. 1–11.

Kennedy, Adrienne, and Werner Sollors. *The Adrienne Kennedy Reader.* University of Minnesota Press, 2001.

Stephens, Judith L. "Anti-Lynch Plays by African American Women: Race, Gender, and Social Protest in American Drama." *African American Review,* vol. 26, no. 2, Summer 1992, pp. 329–339.

NOTE

1 Portions of this introduction are taken from the *for colored girls* ... program note that I wrote for Kansas City Repertory Theatre in 2019.

CHAPTER 2

Staging Queer Feminisms and Legacies in North America

Bess Rowen

As Paula Vogel once said, "In the work of every American playwright at the end of the 20th century, there are only two stages: before she has read Maria Irene Fornes—and after" (The Free Library). Alisa Solomon repeated this quote in the obituary she wrote following Fornés's death in 2018, and it is Solomon's book that sparked the collaboration that resulted in Vogel's play, *Indecent*. Even this small example shows the web of connections and impact that these two important queer women playwrights, theatrical innovators, and mentors continue to have in the American theatre. Fornés and Vogel both spurred important shifts in how plays are written and staged through works such as Fornés's *Promenade* (1965), *Fefu and Her Friends* (1977), and *And What of the Night?* (1990) and Vogel's *The Baltimore Waltz* (1992), *How I Learned to Drive* (1997), and *Indecent* (2015). But beyond these innovative plays, Fornés and Vogel have trained and mentored generations of influential North American playwrights including Ayad Akhtar, Jordan Harrison, Quiara Alegría Hudes, Tarell Alvin McCraney, Lynn Nottage, Sylvan Oswald, and Sarah Ruhl. The impact of these two figures in the theatrical landscape of the 20th and 21st centuries is even more impressive when so much of it occurred despite limitations that universities and other formal kinds of training created to block queer women from positions of prominence. Fornés and Vogel's queer feminist approaches not only dismantle the patriarchal models of playwriting created by white cisgender, heterosexual men

DOI: 10.4324/9781003272854-3

by staging women's stories in new ways, but also demonstrate new modes of mentorship and community by creating cohorts of talented and creative playwrights with new perspectives.

Although there are many plays that could be used as examples of Fornés and Vogel's innovations, Fornés's *Fefu and Her Friends* and Vogel's *Indecent* present opportunities to chart the response to intersectional queer feminist plays four decades apart. As is the case with any study of marginalized voices within the context of mainstream culture, progress did not occur overnight. Instead, the commercial runs of these Fornés and Vogel plays—and the awards they did or did not win—tell a story about how much queer feminist experimentation the American theatre was ready to see in the late 20th and early 21st centuries. This narrative reveals how much rarer it was, and is, for women with multiple marginalized intersectional identity markers to be given the opportunity to step outside the expected forms of playwriting and play staging; harder for Vogel as a queer woman, but harder still for Fornés as a queer Cuban woman.

As noted in the introduction to this volume, this text purposefully pushes back against the white, patriarchal fallacy of a linear chronology of "milestones," which is particularly useful in this case, as the circumstances surrounding *Fefu and Her Friends* and *Indecent* are not neatly defined. To that end, this chapter follows Fornés and Vogel's examples by focusing on thematic similarities, characters, and context surrounding these two milestone plays written by key figures in the field. The importance of these two works becomes particularly evident when we consider when these plays occurred in the theatrical careers of their respective playwrights as well as their shared interests in both theatrical performance and **gender performativity** and their place in Fornés and Vogel's teaching legacies. This chapter follows those three areas of influence in an attempt to model the queer feminist approaches to theatre-making, teaching, community-building, and creating knowledge that define the legacies of both these important women and their works.

THEATRE IS/IN LIFE: *FEFU* AND *INDECENT* IN CONTEXT

Fornés was already a well-known figure in North American theatre when *Fefu and Her Friends* premiered in New York City in 1977. She was born in Havana, Cuba, in 1931 and moved to America in her teens. By age 20, she was a United States citizen. By age 30, she was a playwright. Fornés first studied visual art, and she credited her romantic relationship with noted queer feminist writer and theorist Susan Sontag as the catalyst for her pivot toward writing. She first garnered critical attention, and her first Off-Broadway Theatre Award (commonly referred to as an Obie Award), with a pair of plays called *The Successful Life of 3* and *Promenade*, with music by Al Carmines. In 1981, she became the head of the Hispanic Playwrights-in-Residence program at **INTAR** (International Arts Relations) in New York City, a position she would hold until 1991. It took until 1990 for her to be named a Pulitzer Prize finalist for *And What of the Night?*, but she never won the award. Fornés continued writing until the effects of Alzheimer's Disease took its toll on her in the early 2000s, and she ultimately succumbed to her illness in 2018. This brief history places *Fefu* in the middle of Fornés's illustrious career—a moment in which the downtown New York theatre scene knew her name, but before she would become known as a master teacher and nationally known theatre-maker.

Despite this chronology, *Fefu* itself sits outside of the rest of Fornés's work. The character-driven story of a woman named Fefu and her seven friends is filled with the incisive and poetic prose that is a staple of her style, but the focus on an informal 1935 get-together of mostly straight, white, middle-class friends preparing a charity presentation is both far from Fornés's own experiences and her usual dramatic fare. The character Fefu often stands in contrast to Julia, a character whose emotional vulnerability is physically echoed by a recent physical injury that requires her to use a wheelchair. No men appear on the stage, although Fefu's husband, Phillip, is ostensibly on the property. There is even a reference to Chekhov's gun,[1] in the guise of Fefu's rifle, which is introduced at the very start of the action and whose firing ends the play with the death of a rabbit and, somewhat mysteriously, Julia.

Yet this account of *Fefu and Her Friends* does not do justice to Fornés's innovations. The play is simultaneously realistic and expressionistic in that it does not have a singular plot, though there are subplots aplenty as the characters discuss topics ranging from gender to art to relationships to pain. The interest in character over plot is also indicative of Fornés's style but, in *Fefu,* this aspect of storytelling is aided by its unique staging. The play takes place in Fefu's house, but not in a single room; rather, the characters often have conversations in different rooms of the house at the same time. When she directed the original production of *Fefu,* Fornés made the decision to divide the staging area into four different rooms with one audience area designated for each portion of the set. The entire audience could see Parts I and III of the play together, but Part II was divided into four simultaneous scenes that were repeated four times each while the entire audience physically moved between scenes, allowing everyone to see each scene but in a different order. Instead of creating a rotating stage, Fornés notably chose to have the audience stand up and move to the next area to continue the play. Using a particular physical location to create the ambiance of a specific scene or play came to be a defining feature of **environmental theatre,** meaning *Fefu* is a milestone production for this form of performance. Despite this creative staging, *Fefu* is unusually realistic for a Fornés play, where one is usually likely to find other pieces of literature and film integrated into the text or episodic structures that disrupt a sense of "real" time, yet it is the play that generally introduces Fornés' name to students of theatre.

Paula Vogel's *Indecent* exists in quite a different moment of its playwright's career. Vogel was born in Washington, DC, in 1951, the same year Fornés became a US citizen. Vogel attended Bryn Mawr in the 1970s—which is the kind of college that Fefu and her friends likely attended—but she actually graduated from Catholic University in Washington, DC, before heading to Cornell for her MA and PhD. Her dissertation topic was meant to be a queer, feminist look at hiding scenes in restoration comedy, but two of her committee members left the university and the remaining faculty members were not amenable to the project. Vogel left Cornell in 1981 without completing her degree. In 2016, with the support of Cornell faculty member Sara Warner, Vogel defended the research contained within her play *Indecent* to complete her doctorate. Thus, *Indecent* is a milestone in Vogel's academic and theatrical career, but one that contains the wisdom of four decades of playwriting experience. Whereas Fornés had to wait another 13 years after *Fefu* to be nominated for a Pulitzer, Vogel won the award for *How I Learned to Drive* in 1998, 17 years prior to *Indecent*.

Indecent tells the story of Sholem Asch's *The God of Vengeance*, another milestone play that marked the first time a lesbian love story was shown on Broadway in 1922. Vogel had first encountered *The God of Vengeance* while at Cornell, but it was only after director and collaborator Rebecca Taichman encountered the play in Alisa Solomon's book, *Re-dressing the Canon: Essays on Theatre and Gender*, that Vogel returned to Asch's work. Asch, a Polish-Jewish author, wrote the play in Yiddish, and it premiered in Berlin in 1907. The play was not controversial in Yiddish when it first came to the United States, but, when it was translated and moved to Broadway, its portrayal of Jewish people as brothel-owners, sex workers, and queer women scared middle-class Jewish Americans who were aiming at assimilation. In one rather astonishing scene, sex worker Manke asks the brothel-owner's daughter, Rifkele, to play in the rain with her; the two frolic in the rain and pretend to be bride and groom before they share a romantic kiss. After the Rabbi at Temple Emanu-El synagogue reported the play for indecency, the producers and the cast were indicted. In the end, the producers paid a fine and the play was not shut down. In *Indecent*, Vogel shifted some of these circumstances slightly for dramatic effect, but Vogel's iteration follows the controversy surrounding *The God of Vengeance* and repeats its rain scene in several different circumstances: from an initial reading to a fully enacted scene performed in Yiddish, by which time the audience no longer needs translation. The action is shown through a troupe and stage manager who literally rise from the ashes to bring the story's multiple time periods to life.

Although *Indecent* marks neither the initial high point of Vogel's career nor its end, the play is notable because it marked

Fig. 2.1 Mimi Lieber, Max Gordon Moore, Adina Verson, Katrina Lenk, and Tom Nelis in Paula Vogel's *Indecent*, directed by Rebecca Taichman, La Jolla Playhouse, San Diego, CA, 2015. Photo by Jim Carmody.

both her Broadway debut and her dissertation. *Indecent* also signals a return to Vogel's interest in memory plays that take a collective approach to staging past events, here with the collective trauma of the Holocaust as opposed to the individual trauma of sexual assault and incest in *How I Learned to Drive*. *Indecent* also joins *The Baltimore Waltz*—Vogel's love letter to her brother, Carl, who died of AIDS—in the sense that both plays revolve around a large moment of loss for the LGBTQ community. *Indecent* combines these themes of memory across collective trauma and loss as it reinscribes the realities of queer Jewish women into the narrative of the Holocaust, serving as a reminder that queer Jewish women existed and that their stories did (and do) matter.

"WE HAVE A STORY WE WANT TO TELL YOU":[2] QUEER FEMINIST METATHEATRICALITY AND PERFORMATIVITY

Although the circumstances surrounding *Fefu and Her Friends* and *Indecent* differ, both plays use internal theatrical metaphors to challenge gender roles and explore gender constructs through performance. Each play features a different feminist and queer collaborative aesthetic that leads these plays' forms to mimic their functions. Fornés served as her own director for *Fefu*—and for her subsequent plays—because she saw directing as an extension of playwriting. She believed that a singular vision was important for a piece of theatre, although she was open to inspiration from those around her. This attitude leads Penny Farfan to argue that *Fefu* "posits postmodern feminist theatre practice as a constructive response to the psychic dilemmas of the play's female characters" (443; see **postmodern feminism**). The characters in *Fefu* are putting on a play to not only help raise money for their charity, but also to make sense of the differences between where they envisioned their lives going and what the United States in the 1930s was willing to allow women to do. Yet, in both the play and Fornés's own career, the individual energies do not coalesce into a unified voice. This is not the case with Vogel's *Indecent*, which is a collaboration with director Rebecca Taichman and uses collective storytelling via a theatre troupe whose actors perform multiple characters throughout the play. This queer feminist approach to traumatic memory links *Indecent* to a technique Vogel first utilized in *How I Learned to Drive*. Writing about the latter, Ann Pellegrini discusses how *Drive* seems to "link the future of feminism, its revitalization, to a different way of thinking about and encountering feminism's own past" (415). Both these plays stage the pitfalls and possibilities that exist in feminist theatre-making to work through the events of the past and stage the future.

This theme is most obvious in *Indecent*, which opens as a troupe literally rises from the ashes to reperform key moments of *The God of Vengeance* from its original writing in 1907 to its Broadway debut in 1922 until Asch's final years in the 1950s. *Indecent* might begin as a story about the censorship of the play, but it moves quickly to the theme of art as a means of healing collective trauma—in this case, the trauma of the Holocaust. *Indecent* reminds contemporary audiences that theatre can restage forgotten, and erased, histories. Representations of the Holocaust can certainly be found in theatre, but the story of two women in love is not the general focus of those works. The second half of *Indecent* shows *The God of Vengeance* being staged in the Polish ghetto as an escape, a reminder of humanity, and a point of national pride. By staging this story within the world of the play, *Indecent* represents how a theatre can provide comfort in dark times, reminding contemporary audiences of the communal impulse to use performance as a means of both memory and escape. In an interview with Profile Theatre ahead of the New York premiere production, Vogel explains:

> I think about [*Indecent*] as a love story in terrible times. If we love music and theatre and the arts, if we take solace in people sitting beside us in the theatre, if we do what is in our hearts, I think there is light for us. I think the power of us being together in a community that gives us light through the darkness. ("An Interview")

The communities brought together within *Indecent* are not only the acting troupe and the audience, but also those who feel seen in the play's portrayal of art, religion, gender, and sexual orientation.

Although *Indecent* at first seems to be more concerned with sexual orientation than gender, the play begins with Rifkele and Manke being read by men in a Polish literary salon, a mode of gathering that became popular in the 18th and 19th centuries for intellectuals and artists to share their work. The initial queering of these characters comes first from the fact that two men read their lines, which is only heightened when one of the men refuses to continue with the lesbian content. This straight man feels uncomfortable reading aloud lines that reveal an attraction to a woman, even when he is meant to be portraying a woman, which shows how powerful the idea of gender can be within the realm of the play and performance. His refusal to continue leaves narrator/stage manager Lemml to read Rifkele as Asch himself reads Manke. Therefore, it is gender that supplants sexuality as the most visible and important factor in a scene in which three men play two queer women. Later, Lemml goes on to be a champion of the play and the scene itself, ultimately bringing the women to life on stage through his memory. The queer tenderness, consent, and vulnerability present in the rain scene initially sprang from the mind of someone we know as a cisgender, straight man in Sholem Asch, but queer women like Vogel, Taichman, and others see *The God of Vengeance* faithfully representing the nuances of gender and sexuality in these queer Jewish women. This unconventional "conversation" and collaboration between a straight man and queer women, over time, accounts for why the collective within the world of *Indecent* includes men in a sustained and supported way. The allyship of those surrounding the two women lovers over time is a model for the way that theatre creates a community even beyond the people who are the focus of a play's story.

Fefu and Her Friends begins with a provocation concerning femininity through Fefu's famous line: "My husband married me to have a constant reminder of how loathsome women are" (Fornés 7). Later on, Fefu explains liking "men better than women" because "men have natural strength. Women have to find their strength, and when they do find it, it comes forth with bitterness and it's erratic" (15). The staging of gender in this play revolves around the limits of femininity, many of which Fefu transgresses. Much has been made of Fefu's identification with masculinity, her association with the rifle, and of her contrast to the wounded Julia. Although the play stages scenes from the rehearsal of the educational presentation the women have gathered to prepare, it is the language regarding gender that truly performs, in line with Judith Butler's sense of **gender performativity**. Butler argues that gender is comprised of a series of repeated behaviors and actions that are performed for a social audience—which is not to say that gender is "false," but rather that it is an ever-evolving expression in a cultural context. When Julia explains that "the human being is of the masculine gender" (35), she is expressing the way that society reads men as neutral and assumed standard identity. After Julia's first appearance on stage, the other characters comment that she had been fearless before her "accident"—a confusing situation in which a deer was shot and Julia also fell to the ground, later insisting she had been tortured. Julia's vulnerability now stands in for the weakness that Fefu associates with femininity, and Fefu's

Fig. 2.2 Amelia Workman as Fefu, Ronete Levenson as Sue, Jennifer Lim as Cindy, Carmen Zilles as Cecilia, Juliana Canfield as Christina, Lindsay Rico as Paula, Brittany Bradford as Julia in the Theatre for a New Audience (Brooklyn, NY) production of *Fefu and Her Friends* by María Irene Fornés, directed by Lileana Blain-Cruz. Photo by Gerry Goodstein.

shooting of another pastoral animal, this time a rabbit, causes Julia to fall to the ground dead at the play's end. Fefu has killed that which she feared and despised in herself.

Fornés's choice to set the play in the 1930s seemingly draws a parallel between the way culture in the 1930s sought to counteract the relative freedoms afforded to women of the 1920s flapper era in a similar way that the 1970s pushed back against the feminist, civil rights, and queer liberation movements of the 1960s. The women in *Fefu* cannot find fulfillment in a world where even the most privileged (white, wealthy, educated) women have limited career options outside of the home. In response, *Fefu* uses theatrical storytelling, on both the level of the play itself and the rehearsal within the play, to stage creative possibilities that could not find full expression in the real world. Fornés's choices to show Fefu's lack of gender conformity and explicitly mention the former romantic relationship between Paula and Celia is also notable because it is rare to see representations of queer women from a queer woman playwright. Yet, as Gwendolyn Alker and others have noted, Fornés did not foreground her queerness (nor her Cuban identity) in her work, so "the lens of queerness can be applied to Fornés' life and aesthetic, but should also be problematized as a way of understanding her body of work" (Alker 77). Queerness is, indeed, not more pertinent than the feminist collectivity that characters and actors alike require to survive.

"THE CONCERN OF THE EDUCATOR":[3] FORNÉS AND VOGEL'S TEACHING LEGACIES

What do celebrated playwrights Christina Anderson, Ayad Akhtar, Migdalia Cruz, Nilo Cruz, Sarah DeLappe, Gina Gionfriddo, Jordan Harrison, Quiara Alegría Hudes, Stephen Karam, Rajiv Joseph, Eduardo Machado, Tarell Alvin McCraney, Cherríe Moraga, Lynn Nottage, Sylvan Oswald, Sarah Ruhl, and Caridad Svich have in common? They have all studied with Maria Irene Fornés and/or Paula Vogel over the years. While only a small fraction of their students, this list contains an impressive array of individuals who have won Pulitzer Prizes, Obie awards, MacArthur Genius grants, Susan Smith Blackwell prizes, and National Endowment for the Arts fellowships. Many of the most lauded playwrights in North American theatre today have been shaped by Fornés and Vogel. Teaching has not only been important in these two playwrights' careers because their students have won awards, but also because their career trajectories make clear their deep commitments to teaching and mentoring. *Fefu and Her Friends* and *Indecent* also serve as pedagogical tools that model the concerns and techniques of their playwriting.

This connection between theatrical and educational legacies is particularly crucial in understanding Fornés's legacy, as her plays are not performed with the same regularity as Vogel's. As Caridad Svich notes, Fornés's

> force as teacher and mentor has often been the only way her vision has had an opportunity to be visibly expressed

in a country where her work as a playwright has been pushed to the very fringe of theatrical experience. The articulation of her aesthetic has been made manifest in her hands-on work as a teacher, and therefore is an essential, inextricable part of her work as playwright and director. (xxvii–xxviii)

The works of Fornés's former students make several things very clear: her exercises were meant to free the imagination and bypass the ego, she did not allow playwrights to lie (to her or themselves), and her visual arts background manifested in a keen eye for the minute visual details of staging. All of these aspects of her teaching can be seen in *Fefu and Her Friends* and her other plays, but as the most well-known Fornés work, *Fefu* also has the distinction of carrying these lessons far beyond the reach of classrooms and workshops of her lesser-known works.

Fefu follows the first pillar of Fornés's teachings both in its complete form and within the conversation the characters have inside the world of the play. For a playwright best known for avant-garde, genre-bending plays, naturalism is an experiment and a risk. Within Fefu's house, the characters let their imaginations run wild and do not worry much about how their statements, confessions, and provocations will make them look. Fefu's admissions concerning her terrible relationship with her husband simultaneously express her insecurities and her desire to control some part of her life. Julia's insistence that she was tortured, even when she knows that some of her friends doubt her story, is another instance of foregrounding the imaginative truth over the management of self-image. Yet individual truths are championed over collective truths in this play, returning to Fornés's idea of the need for an artist to have a singular vision that they do not compromise for the comfort or taste of others. The second aspect of Fornés's technique follows seamlessly, as the harsh truths in this play buck stereotypical gender roles specifically because Fornés neither lies about who these characters are nor shields the audience from their true natures. This commitment to truth also extends to the reality of the visual worlds of her plays. Many who have directed Fornés's works speak about the practicality of their discussions with her about how to, for example, create a realistic dead rabbit prop for Fefu to enter with at the end of the play.

Finally, Fornés's plays often comment on the nature of teaching itself. Indeed, the title of this section comes from a line *Fefu* says at the start of Part III, after the audience is united once again. Cecilia begins the scene by saying each person has their own way of taking in new information and processing it before she states, "That is, I feel, the concern of the educator— to teach how to be sensitive to the differences in ourselves as well as outside ourselves, not to supervise the memorization of facts" (44). This opinion seems to align Cecilia's views on education with Fornés's. Teaching—for Cecilia as well as Fornés—is about helping a student self-actualize as a person and an artist. In this way, *Fefu* follows Susan Sontag's assessment that "character is revealed through catechism. People requiring or giving instruction is a standard situation in Fornés's plays. The desire to be initiated, to be taught, is depicted as an essential, and essentially pathetic, longing" (18). The women in *Fefu* have had the benefit of formal education and economic security, yet they debate the purpose and use of that education throughout the play. Still, despite the ambivalence expressed within plays like *Fefu* about the process of education, Fornés never stopped teaching and learning. Indeed, *Fefu and Her Friends* not only discusses some of Fornés's pedagogical ideas, but also exemplifies them by showing what a playwright with a unique vision can accomplish when she is empowered to bring her own play to life.

The idea of a play modeling a kind of theatre-making for a playwright's students also applies to *Indecent*. In an interview with Daniel Pollack-Penzer for *The New Yorker*, Vogel called the play "a love letter to all her students who dare to write incendiary plays" that unsettle people for a purpose. Vogel certainly knew about how to create meaningful discomfort, as shown by her great critical successes such as *How I Learned to Drive*. That play concerns grooming, sexual assault of a minor, and incest, but it also takes incredible pains to spare the actors from needing to retell traumatic parts of this story, particularly in the part of the play's protagonist, Li'l Bit.

Indecent returns to the concerns of memory, trauma, and community, but comes to a different conclusion than Vogel's Pulitzer Prize-winning play of almost two decades prior. The Vogel of *Drive* is more interested in the process of individual trauma, while the skilled teacher Vogel of *Indecent* focuses on the ways that community, particularly theatrical community, can help make people feel seen, important, and powerful when society has seemingly forgotten them. In her Profile Theatre interview, Vogel noted that the play is less about the obscenity trial and more "about a fiery young playwright—not just Asch, but me, too—ignored for decades and then embraced by students." Seen from this perspective, *Indecent*'s success is somewhat ironic. The play expressing frustration of what, and who, is ignored or forgotten ended up reigniting interest in Vogel and Asch, creating a new vogue for readings and productions of *The God of Vengeance* and *Indecent* alike.

As for Vogel, *Indecent* not only reignited the theatre industry's interest in Vogel—garnering a Broadway transfer and nominations for Obie, Drama Desk, and Tony Awards for Best Play—but also earned Vogel the educational and research recognition that comes with a PhD, even after she had been abandoned within her dissertation process. Although Vogel taught in some of the most prestigious theatre programs at major universities throughout her career, her lack of a terminal degree (in theatre, a PhD or MFA) certainly impacted her place within the formal academy in terms of both job security and compensation level. But, unlike Fornés, Vogel's impact as a teacher and mentor is something that is recognized by the popular press in addition to the inner circle of theatre-makers and teachers. Within student descriptions of her work are some familiar forms of praise—they speak of her dedication to a playwright's unique theatrical voice, her interest in the visual world of the play, and her experimentation with what theatricality can and will be. Clearly, Fornés and Vogel both have distinct styles of writing plays and of teaching playwriting, but their interests in both the lyrical and visual aspects of staging stories share those principles. Vogel's students also speak of the ways that her visual interest in a play extends to the realm of the written playscript as well. The physical form of her works, and her students' works, on the printed page reveal a sensibility that links the experience of reading of plays to the imaginative worlds that staging them will bring. This is true not only in the physical format of the scripts, but also in the way that elements like stage directions are used to increase and impart theatricality.

One of the most important aspects of watching *Indecent* comes from the use of projected titles, which not only clarify location and language, but also share some of Vogel's stage directions with the audience. At the start of the play, the troupe rises from the ashes, which is achieved by having dust pour out of the actors' sleeves and clothes. In a certain sense, Vogel too was rising from the ashes, a phoenix. Her Broadway premiere occurred in the same season as her student Lynn Nottage's first Broadway production. Nottage would go on to win her second Pulitzer for that play, *Sweat*, which also includes slips in time and features people who historical narratives often forget: the blue-collar workers in a small steel town. Both *Sweat* and *Indecent* took on new, powerful resonance during Donald Trump's presidency in 2017, where the least visible portions of the population seemed to consist of both the most vulnerable and the biggest threats to democracy.

"PLEASE DON'T LET THIS BE THE ENDING":4 STAGING QUEER FEMINIST FUTURES

In the years since 2020, both *Fefu and Her Friends* and *Indecent* have been frequent choices in theatrical seasons as North America continues to grapple with a conservative backlash against bodily autonomy for women, LGBTQIA+ people, and BIPOC people. In these two plays, Fornés and Vogel stage worlds that reveal important truths about the ways in which society is ill-equipped for people who do not fit white, cis-hetero patriarchal norms. These two plays set in the early 20th century still resonate for people living a century later than their characters. In fact, it is impossible to conclude a discussion about Maria Irene Fornés and Paula Vogel, whose works are still so alive, pressing, and evolving. These two works are milestones in theatre because of their unique stagings, their celebration of hidden herstories, and their willingness to hold a mirror up to a society that still has far to go to reach truly intersectional feminist ideals of equity. Fornés and Vogel are pillars of queer feminist theatre, but those are not the only arenas in which they operate. Their legacies will continue through the work of their students, through the work of their students' students, and so on. And years from this moment, people will watch a play whose lineage can be traced back to these theatrical innovators. Fornés and Vogel are not only part of queer feminist theatre's past, but a part of its present and rich future as well. In *Indecent,* when Lemml is afraid that the Holocaust is the end of *God of Vengeance*'s story, he closes his eyes and frees Manke and Rifkele from the line at the gas chambers. Indeed, art lives as long as it is useful, which means that this chapter must stop long before the end of these two illustrious careers.

FURTHER RESOURCES

Delgado, Maria M., and Caridad Svich, eds. *Conducting a Life: Reflections on the Theatre of Maria Irene Fornes.* Smith & Kraus, 1999.
This edited volume forms a textual collage of Fornés's legacy. The interviews, essays, reflections, and materials in this collection show Fornés's many sides and manages to capture both her teaching style and her personality. The pages simulate what it would be like to sit in on one of Fornés's classes or rehearsals.
Farfan, Penny. "Feminism, Metatheatricality, and Mise-en-Scene in Maria Irene Fornes's *Fefu and Her Friends.*" *Modern Drama,* vol. 40, no. 4 (1997), pp. 442–453.
This excellent essay not only covers the connection between dramaturgy and mise-en-scène in *Fefu,* but also serves as a detailed microhistory of this milestone play. Farfan discusses the themes, Fornés's direction, and the connections to Fornés's earlier works.
Jones, Lee Brewer. *Paula Vogel: Practice, Pedagogy, and Influences.* Methuen Press, 2023.
This volume takes up important intersections in Vogel's ever-expanding career. Jones is particularly interested in the intersection of Vogel's writing and teaching. It includes recent works and detailed analyses of her impact as playwright and mentor.
Pollack-Pelzner, Daniel. "With Her Eerily timely 'Indecent,' Paula Vogel Unsettles American Theatre Again" *The New Yorker,* 12 May 2017, https://www.newyorker.com/books/page-turner/

with-her-eerily-timely-indecent-paula-vogel-unsettles-american-theatre-again. Accessed January 3, 2024.

This in-depth interview charts Vogel's relationship to *The God of Vengeance*, Rebecca Taichman, Cornell, and her teaching career. There are remarkably few pieces charting how *Indecent* is connected to Vogel's academic career, making this particularly notable.

Robinson, Marc. *The Theater of Maria Irene Fornes*. Johns Hopkins University Press, 1999.

This collection of essays provides a supplement to an earlier volume from two years prior. This collection has essays on the plays and production processes from a variety of scholars and artists and then a final section of Fornés's own writings. Together, they form a picture of this multifaceted artist who was closer to the end of her professional career than anyone could have imagined.

REFERENCES

Alker, Gwendolyn. "Maria Irene Fornes." *50 Key Figures in Queer US Theatre*. Ed. Jimmy Noriega and Jordan Schildcrout. Routledge, 2022, pp. 76–80.

"An Interview with the Playwright: Paula Vogel on *Indecent*" https://vineyardtheatre.org/archive/interview-playwright-paula-vogel-indecent/. Accessed January 10, 2024.

Farfan, Penny. "Feminism, Metatheatricality, and Mise-en-Scene in Maria Irene Fornes's *Fefu and Her Friends*." *Modern Drama*, vol. 40, no. 4, 1997, pp. 442–453.

Fornés, Maria Irene. *Fefu and Her Friends*. PAJ Publications, 1990.

The Free Library. "Her Championship Season." https://www.thefreelibrary.com/Her+championship+season.-a057155932. Accessed November 15, 2022.

Pellegrini, Ann. "Staging Sexual Injury: *How I Learned to Drive*." *Critical Theory and Performance: Revised and Enlarged Edition*. Ed. Janelle Reinelt and Joseph Roach. University of Michigan Press, 2007.

Pollack-Pelzner, Daniel. "With her Eerily Timely 'Indecent,' Paula Vogel Unsettles American Theatre Again," *The New Yorker*, May 12, 2017. https://www.newyorker.com/books/page-turner/with-her-eerily-timely-indecent-paula-vogel-unsettles-american-theatre-again. Accessed November 30, 2022.

Sontag, Susan. "A Preface to the Plays of Maria Irene Fornés." *The Theater of Maria Irene Fornés*. Ed. Marc Robinson. Johns Hopkins University Press, 1999, pp. 43–46.

Svich, Caridad, and Delgado, Maria M., editors. *Conducting a Life: Reflections on the Theatre of Maria Irene Fornes*, Smith & Kraus, 1999. Vogel, Paula. *Indecent*. New York: Theatre Communications Group, 2017.

NOTES

1 Playwright Anton Chekhov wrote that placing a gun onstage in the first act must result in it firing in later acts. It need not be a real gun and can refer to any element introduced specifically to build tension into the story when it returns later. In *Fefu*, it is a literal gun.
2 Vogel 10.
3 Fornes 44.
4 Vogel 73.

CHAPTER 3

Making Lesbian-Feminist Theatre

Lois Weaver, Tammy WhyNot, and the Legacy of Split Britches

Benjamin Gillespie

Lois Weaver has been a leading performer, director, and teacher for more than four decades. As a lesbian and feminist, she has long centered her artistic practice on her own identity and desires. More recently, her work has focused on the intersection of her lesbian-feminist identity with the aging process in her numerous performance projects. As co-founder of Split Britches, one of the longest-running theatre companies in the US, Weaver has continuously challenged traditional gender roles, confronted patriarchal values, and defied heterosexual imperatives, most notably through the contrast of **butch/femme** lesbian roleplay on stage—a hallmark of 1980s feminist performance and lesbian subculture that continues to be foregrounded in her work. This chapter analyzes Weaver's legacy as a lesbian-feminist performer, both with Split Britches and through the use of her alter ego Tammy WhyNot, a performance persona she developed in the late 1970s which she has continued to perform today to address difficult conversations with her audiences and to act as host in her Public Address Systems community projects. Tracking the legacy and development of Lois Weaver and Tammy WhyNot simultaneously showcases the history of lesbian-feminist performance from the early days of the WOW Café Theatre up to the present day.

Co-founded by Lois Weaver, Peggy Shaw, and Deb Margolin in 1981, Split Britches is known for creating original works

 DOI: 10.4324/9781003272854-4

that deconstruct canonical "straight" plays, novels, and other texts, including Tennessee Williams's *A Streetcar Named Desire*, Louisa May Alcott's *Little Women*, and popular films from *Dr. Strangelove* to *Marriage Story*. Split Britches use personal stories as fodder for performance, often blending theatre and life on stage by layering themselves with only a thin veneer of character traits. The troupe's work is calculatedly postmodern, queer, and **metatheatrical**—as far away from realism as possible, and for good reason. As feminist scholar Elin Diamond has fervently argued, historically the genre of realism often has negative outcomes for both the representation of women and queer people, thus it is not surprising that lesbian-feminist theatre rejected this style from the beginning. This was one of the main arguments made in Diamond's influential book, *Unmaking Mimesis: Essays on Feminism and Theatre* (1997). As Diamond recognizes, Split Britches has always been proudly working-class, lesbian, and feminist—an intersectional formation that has characterized the troupe's work for over forty-five years.

As a founding member of Split Britches, Weaver's sexy femme lesbian stage presence opposite Shaw's butch lesbian persona exemplifies the New York City-based lesbian-feminist theatre movement of the early 1980s. In this period, a diverse group of women artists—primarily queer women—came together to form a community that focused on voicing concerns about patriarchal and homophobic culture as well as staging and exploring the taboo subjects of lesbian sex and desire. While there were many women's theatre groups dispersed around the United States by the late 1970s, it was in October 1980 that Weaver and Shaw created the Women's One World Festival, which brought together many lesbian women performers in New York City. At the festival, Shaw, Weaver, and Margolin premiered *Split Britches*, a production that ultimately gave the company its provocative name. While Margolin remained active in the troupe until the early 1990s, Shaw and Weaver have remained its primary members up to present day, producing solo and co-performed works under this celebrated moniker. The Women's One World festival featured performances from a growing community of women interested in exploring lesbian joy, love, and sex on stage—creating theatre by and for women in a culture dominated by men. The popularity and success of the festival eventually led to the development of a dedicated performance space called the WOW Café Theatre, first located on the Lower East Side in 1981. As spokespersons for the larger lesbian community surrounding them, Weaver and Shaw led the creative charge to find a venue to house lesbian work, leading to the beginning of WOW. Without an appointed Artistic Director, WOW was (and is) a collective run by members of its ever-shifting community of women. While the venue has moved from its original location, it is still in operation today, now located in the East Village and remaining the longest collectively-run women's and trans-inclusive performance space in the US.

At WOW, Weaver, Shaw, and other artists were able to experiment freely with different performance styles while exploring personal identity on stage. Their performances generated some of the most groundbreaking theatre of the late 20th century, inspiring a period of feminist theatre scholarship that changed the field of theatre and performance studies. Led by feminist scholars such as Sue-Ellen Case, Jill Dolan, and Kate Davy, interventions in scholarship and performance created space for and documented theatre created by women through an explicitly lesbian-feminist aesthetic. According to Davy, WOW was a theatre space that presumed a lesbian worldview: "In this context, WOW artists create a theatre for lesbians, a theatre that responds to lesbian subjectivity" (137). Not only was the WOW Café Theatre created out of the desire to explore and foreground lesbian identity, but it also challenged the sexism embedded in theatre institutions and practices more broadly through its women-centered programming and coterie audiences. According to Davy, in its earlier days,

> WOW performances efface a heterosexual address by constructing a spectator who is neither a man nor a woman, but a lesbian—a subject defined in terms of sexual similarity. Same-sexuality is the model and organizing principle from which WOW artists work. (138)

Challenging gender *and* sexual norms was at the forefront of the WOW aesthetic and the lesbian-feminist theatre movement more broadly.

Weaver, an outspoken and visibly femme lesbian, was one of WOW's most ardent voices alongside Shaw. The butch/femme role-play and heightened sexual dynamic of the duo on stage was central to the lesbian turn in feminist discourse of this period (where their work is repeatedly cited), and the creation of the postmodern, do-it-yourself approach embraced at WOW as a working-class theatre. Both Shaw and Weaver took a sex-radical position to undermine a homophobic feminist discourse, centering sexual seduction over gender dynamics and differences between men and women. While too complex for a full explanation here, the theoretical debates between straight and lesbian feminists of the time around issues of gender and sexuality partially led to the development of queer theory in the 1990s, especially through the work of Judith Butler (1990). The new visibility of lesbian subjectivity on and off stage inspired debates theorizing butch/femme lesbian sexuality that Split Britches epitomized.

Butch/femme gender roles refer to the performance of masculine and feminine identity in lesbian subcultures as expressed through the body, clothing, erotic desires, and role-playing—or what Butler calls *gender performativity*—in an explicitly lesbian context. Rather than simply challenging the gender binary, butch/femme sexuality exists beyond the confines of a male-dominated culture to make lesbian subjectivity visible on and off stage. As Jill Dolan argues,

> In the lesbian context, playing with fantasies of sexual and gender roles offers the potential for changing gender-coded structures of power. Power is not inherently male; a woman who assumes a dominant role is only male-like if the culture considers power as a solely male attribute. (164)

Butch is not simply an *imitation* of male masculinity, but a subversive reimagining of power within an explicitly lesbian sexual identity. In this pairing, the femme woman is conscious of her own performance of femininity and the gender role of "woman," undermining heterosexual objectification through the visible *desiring* of her butch counterpart. This conceit is central to Split Britches' performances as they draw from popular "straight" plays, films, and television shows, adapting them to challenge **heteronormative** culture. Men are removed altogether from the stage picture, representing, as Dolan observes, the "subversion of the dominant culture's gender-polarized images of sexual power in the context of lesbian desire" (164). In short, butch/femme identities undermine both gendered and sexualized paradigms of heteronormative theatre *and* society, substituting "straight" images with purposefully "deviant" ones that seek to empower rather than suppress both the lesbian performer and her beholder (i.e. the spectator). As Davy argues, butch/femme "is a manifestation of the separation of sexuality from polarized gender constructs and imperative sexuality" (139).

The WOW Café Theatre allowed for the *explicit* articulation and presentation of lesbian desire that positioned gender and sexuality outside of a binary gender system which presumed heterosexuality and patriarchal (male) dominance. Through performances by Weaver, Shaw, and others including Holly Hughes, Carmelita Tropicana, and Moe Angelos and Lisa Kron (two of the Five Lesbian Brothers, another prominent lesbian-feminist performance group), the dynamics of desire shifted to make visible the variance of gender performances on a wider continuum of masculine and feminine roleplay without the presence of men. While Shaw has often imitated butch male crooners like Frank Sinatra and Leonard Cohen during her career, Weaver repeatedly imitated the "high femme" country singer Tammy Wynette through her alter ego Tammy WhyNot, a fictional character she has embodied since the late 1970s.

In "Towards a Butch-Femme Aesthetic," Sue-Ellen Case argues that butch/femme is the lesbian-feminist answer to gay male camp performance—a genre which often erases women while parodying them. Case states, "butch-femme roles evade the notion of 'the female body' as it predominates in feminist theory . . . the female body, the male gaze, and the structures of realism are only sex toys for the butch-femme couple" (46). The presence and performance of lesbian desire challenges the sexist representation of women in both straight and gay male performance, unbinding female subjectivity from the **male gaze**—a term first coined by feminist film theorist Laura Mulvey in 1975. Subverting the male gaze and creating new perspectives at WOW set the stage for Split Britches' decades-long project of undermining gender and sexuality norms *and* for the establishment of a lesbian-feminist theatre criticism. For example, Jill Dolan's pathbreaking *The Feminist Spectator as Critic* (1988) responds to the work she saw at WOW, especially the work of Split Britches, demonstrating how practice directly influenced feminist theory of the period. As a lesbian spectator, Dolan argued that the positionality and identity of the spectator was just as important to consider as the performer, especially in a space like WOW where being lesbian was a given, contrasting most mainstream theatre and culture where the presumed spectator was male. Drawing on Mulvey, Dolan contended that WOW provided a space for a radical feminist spectator to break through the barriers of sexist representation central to other mainstream American theatre by challenging the imperative of a male gaze.

From the beginning, Split Britches embraced a working-class approach to theatre-making by performing, directing, and producing their own work. In fact, the name "Split Britches" is a reference to trousers worn by women while working in farm fields that allowed them to urinate without stopping their labor—a comment on their own working-class backgrounds and the unrecognized labor of theatre-making itself. They also foreground lesbian sexuality and desire, as evidenced by their Artistic Statement (Split Britches, "About"). Split Britches' performances do not rely on conventional plots or linear structures, but instead reflect a postmodern blending of divergent theatrical styles, bringing together vaudeville, cabaret, slapstick comedy, and drag, providing a unique aesthetic legacy in the history of US theatre. Gender-bending roleplay is at the center of the company's celebrated early works, including *Split Britches* (1980/81), *Beauty and the Beast* (1982), *Upwardly Mobile Home* (1984), *Dress Suits to Hire* (with

Holly Hughes) (1987), *Little Women: The Tragedy* (1988), *Anniversary Waltz* (1990), *Belle Reprieve* (1991), *Lesbians Who Kill* (1992), as well as solo works such as Weaver's *Faith and Dancing* (1996) and Shaw's *Menopausal Gentleman* (1996). Four decades after its inception, Shaw and Weaver continue working under the Split Britches name, creating duo and solo-performed works that expand their lesbian-feminist aesthetic developed in their early years at WOW. Recently, Weaver and Shaw have focused on topics related to aging and disability, especially following the stroke Shaw endured in 2011 that left her unable to memorize new material, captured in her solo show *Ruff* (2012/2013), co-written and directed by Weaver. Now both in their mid-seventies, Shaw and Weaver's most recent co-performed works include *Lost Lounge* (2009), *Unexploded Ordnances (UXO)* (2018), and *Last Gasp* (2020/2022), representing an expansion of their participatory approach honed during their early days at WOW.

WHY TAMMY, WHY NOT? CONSTRUCTING LOIS WEAVER'S LESBIAN-FEMINIST ALTER EGO

Weaver originally created alter ego Tammy WhyNot for a production with Spiderwoman Theatre in the late 1970s and continued to resurrect this character through both the WOW Café Theatre and Split Britches. She continues to embody her today as a reminder of her trailblazing efforts as a feminist performance artist, director, activist, and mentor/teacher to multiple generations of feminist and queer artists and audiences. As Tammy, Weaver channels country music legend Tammy Wynette, the "First Lady of Country Music," who reached the height of her fame during the late 1960s and 1970s. In Split Britches fashion, Weaver queerly refashions Wynette through a heightened camp aesthetic in her work, adding a fictional backstory that the once infamous country singer became a lesbian performance artist ("Tammy WhyNot"). The parallel between Lois and Tammy is not lost on audiences.

Weaver was born in 1949 in the Blue Ridge Mountains of Roanoke, Virginia. Her work reflects her 1950s and early 1960s upbringing in the conservative South within a working-class, Baptist home. Weaver was informed by the colonial history of Virginia and witnessing racial discrimination, gender inequality, and homophobia. She frequently draws on this past in her creative practice, including the women who raised her and the customs she learned as a child, especially the importance of Southern hospitality and domestic care. Indeed, her role in performances—especially recently—has been to act as a *host* for her audiences and co-performers. In 1973, Weaver moved to New York City; just three years later, she joined Spiderwoman Theater, founded by Muriel Miguel. Here, Weaver created Tammy, a character who is not *not* Lois Weaver—a playful reality highlighted in her playful fictional surname, "WhyNot." Weaver first conceived of Tammy in 1977 for *The Lysistrata Numbah!* in which she adapted Wynette's country ballad "Stand *by* Your Man" as "Stand *on* Your Man" (Split Britches, "Tammy WhyNot"). Tammy was conceived of as one of the Spartan women, or the "country" women alongside the Athenian "city" women in Spiderwoman's adaptation of Aristophanes' ancient Greek comedy, *Lysistrata*. While later touring Europe with Spiderwoman, Weaver met Shaw, who was also touring in Europe, but with the New York-based drag troupe Hot Peaches. When Shaw and Weaver returned to New York in 1978, they performed briefly with Spiderwoman before forming Split Britches in 1981 to focus more explicitly on lesbian sexuality in performance. Tammy would perennially return in later work, first in Split Britches' *Upwardly Mobile Home* (1984), and later in *What Tammy Needs to Know About Getting Old and Having Sex* (2014/2015), among other appearances, especially in Weaver's various community-based engagement projects called "Public Address Systems". These are a series of public-facing projects about care-centered performance protocols that create alternative spaces for hospitable and critical questioning and collective engagement for marginalized communities. These protocols include The Long Table, Porch Sitting, Care Café, and most recently, the Situation Room. The Tammy persona that Weaver takes on while leading these protocols allows her to engage in difficult topics with audiences and collaborators who might otherwise feel too uncomfortable to engage with, especially surrounding aging sexuality. For Weaver, Tammy "facilitates public engagement and promotes subversive expertise as methods of activism" (Split Britches, "Tammy WhyNot").

As Weaver has frequently noted, intimacy is something she has felt uncomfortable discussing in a public forum (Weaver and Clark). The Tammy persona gives Weaver the ability to engage in deeply personal collaborations, exposing the hidden desires or fears harbored by her collaborators and audiences and engaging with them collectively in preparation for performance. Beyond sexual intimacy, Weaver's work explores how matters supposedly considered "private" might become public and shows how these feelings might be experienced on a larger collective level rather than isolated to the individual level, including feelings of desire, love, friendship, and sex, but also the epidemic of loneliness for older communities.

Despite not having a penchant for country music, Weaver originally imagined the role as a blonde, big-haired country singer with a Southern drawl, but with one major difference: *she would be queer*. Pulling from her distaste for the conservatism of the US South, she exaggerated the persona of Wynette by drawing upon her own femme lesbian identity, also crucial to her dynamic opposite Shaw in Split Britches. As queer legend has it, in the first performance of *The Lysistrata Numbah!* in 1977, Spiderwoman's costumes did not arrive and the company borrowed costumes from the New York-based drag troupe Hot Peaches, which meant the performance was high-femme and glamorous—something Weaver would continue to embrace with Tammy going forward. Tammy allowed Weaver to say what she wanted without fear of the unknown. Of course, Tammy and Weaver share one body, but Tammy's over-the-top persona allows Weaver to engage in conversations and performances she might otherwise fear navigating. As Sue-Ellen Case states, "Tammy is both a country-western star, and the deconstruction of such a persona. She is the performer who exploits and is exploited by her persona" (*Split Britches* 23). Several years later, Tammy was "born again"—an apt play on words harkening back to her Christian Southern upbringing—in Split Britches' *Upwardly Mobile Home* (1984), set in a caravan under the Brooklyn

Bridge. Weaver performed as Tammy, the lead singer of the band "Tammy WhyNot and the Expectations," living with her other family members Mom (played by Shaw) and Levine (played by Margolin).

Upwardly Mobile Home (1984) is a play about a traveling theatre company who are also a queer family. During the Reagan era of the 1980s, New York City was gentrifying so quickly that the homeless populating grew exponentially. The idea for the piece came from a 1983 article in *Rolling Stone* about a contest in Allentown, Pennsylvania, where whoever camped out longest on a billboard won a mobile home: "This show is dedicated to survivors of all depression [and] to all the ways that art grows out through the cracks of poverty and need" (Case, *Split Britches* 22). In the piece, the trio live under the Brooklyn Bridge as they prepare for a performance of the play *The Shanghai Gesture* (1926) by John Colton. The performance features monologues from each character interspersed with dialogue, musical numbers, and metatheatrical performances. Tammy attempts to peddle her clothing to make some money while Mom and Levine try to prepare to perform for audiences. However, Tammy does not want to be in the show and would prefer to sing country ballads or a musical with revival songs. Without running water or reliable food sources, the play showcases the coping strategies of the working class to get by and how outcasts find solace in alternative forms of family.

This is a play within a play within a play created as cheaply as possible. As Mom says in the play, "Life imitates Art." Tammy replies:

> Sometimes I'm afraid we're just too far gone. I'm afraid we just slipped through a crack somewhere and we're drifting out there, so far out there we'll never come back and nobody knows about us; nobody cares or even comes to see us. It's like we're living on the wrong side of the tracks. And I get so tired of waitin' for someone to bring us what we hav'ta have. I get depressed when there's no toilet paper. (106)

Fig. 3.1 (L to R): Lois Weaver (as Tammy WhyNot), Peggy Shaw (as Mom), and Deb Margolin (as Levine) in *Upwardly Mobile Home* (1984). Photo by Eva Weiss. Courtesy Split Britches.

Tammy desires a better life for herself, one where she is a star and has a dedicated audience. She fantasizes about this in the play frequently and attempts to steal the show, even having the other characters perform a number as her backup singers as "Tammy and the Expectations." Indeed, Tammy has *great* expectations for something better, but the real world stops her from getting what she wants. In *Upwardly Mobile Home*, Tammy gives Weaver the distance to explore uncomfortable and contested categories of "trailer trash" vs. "high femme." As she says in the play about her own clothing, "It's not junk, I use it myself!" (94).

Tammy is a comically naïve counterpart to Weaver's more directorial and methodical creative mind. She is a self-proclaimed non-expert who "encourages people to engage in dialogue on difficult questions on the basis of curiosity and desire rather than conventional understandings of expertise" ("Tammy WhyNot"). Decades after her creation, Weaver would go on to develop full-length performances using the Tammy persona, engaging with various topics in the *What Tammy Needs to Know* series (2004–06), an internationally touring solo show. In these performances, Weaver developed her approach of foregrounding audiences *as* her collaborators and co-investigators that would go on to form her later Tammy-centered performances. In *What Tammy Found Out* (2012–13), a performance that doubled as her inaugural lecture as Professor of Contemporary Performance at Queen Mary University of London, UK, Weaver presented her research *as* Tammy, solidifying the influence of her alter ego on the development of her performance pedagogy. As Weaver states, "the overarching aim . . . was to use the persona of Tammy to slowly transform the audience from passive viewer to active participant in a lively discussion on the sharing of skills and experience as a form of education." ("Tammy Whynot"). This collaboration with the audience harkens back to the early WOW days, where Weaver relied on the community to develop the content of Split Britches' performances.

The most recent installment of the series, *What Tammy Needs to Know About Getting Old and Having Sex* (2014–15) was created over a lengthy period and included collaborations with older people living in care homes in the US, UK, and elsewhere. Weaver drew directly upon personal experiences shared by the participants in the care homes as well as Weaver's experience of sex and aging. With more than 45 years on stage, lesbian sexuality is still at the forefront of Weaver's work, but now she is dealing with the taboo of *aging* sexuality. As Weaver states in the performance:

> Now that I'm an aging lesbian southern woman, I want to make that the materials for my work, and I want to look at those stereotypes and explore them, embody and explode them, and make that possible for a lot of other people. (Weaver, *What Tammy Needs to Know*)

In the New York version of *What Tammy Needs to Know About Getting Old and Having Sex,* which premiered at La

MaMa in 2014, Weaver engaged with four local senior care centers, collaborating with residents to devise the performance collectively. She describes the piece as an "international, intergenerational mission to ask all the difficult questions, talk to those who really know and find out the truth about sex, and all its associations, at midlife and beyond" ("Tammy WhyNot"). The La MaMa production was part talk show, part comeback tour, part exposé on elder sex. It included nearly a dozen elder collaborators of all genders, races, and ages ranging from their mid-sixties to mid-eighties all living in care homes in New York City. It also featured nine full-length original songs intermixed among popular songs with altered lyrics—another hallmark of the Split Britches aesthetic. The musical numbers are shuffled between monologues and talk show-esque interview segments conducted by Tammy as participants tell stories about their sex lives.

Like all of Split Britches' past work, *What Tammy Needs to Know About Getting Old and Having Sex* is nonlinear and episodic. At the top of the show, Weaver appears as Tammy sitting on stage in bare feet with an oversized blonde wig on her head tied up by a polka-dotted bright pink scarf. She wears snakeskin-printed leggings and a white T-shirt with an animated image of a vulva. She sits on a pink yoga mat (a seemingly universal sign of wellness) and puts on a wireless microphone. Shaw enters from stage left as the "Stage Manager" to announce to the audience that this is a concert rehearsal. She performs a sound check—a hilarious metatheatrical moment, especially at La MaMa where Shaw and Weaver have performed hundreds of shows.

Tammy/Weaver begins her monologue with a heightened Southern drawl: "I don't know about all of y'all, but sometimes I don't feel like it!" (Weaver, *What Tammy Needs to Know*), setting the stage for the numerous double entendres to come. She discusses the energy and labor it takes to get herself ready for a public appearance, speaking directly to the audience: "I want to know, after all these years if you might know who I am. Or if you know how I feel or how I think. Or if you still want my body . . . *Anybody*?" (Ibid.).

Fig. 3.2 Lois Weaver as Tammy Whynot. Photo by Christa Holka. Courtesy Split Britches.

This inherent focus on beauty and aging is part of a larger cultural obsession with the preservation of the body through anti-aging campaigns that Weaver is clearly attempting to subvert. As she finishes her monologue, the first song begins: a banjo plays over the speaker and morphs into a campy rendition of Justin Timberlake's 2006 pop hit "Sexy Back," with Weaver changing the words to apply to her own experience of growing older while dancing comically for her multigenerational audience.

As Weaver concludes the song, she picks up a bright pink blazer with "Tammy" emblazoned in sequins on the back. She dances for the audience and calls out her co-performers, all from the care home residences in New York, to enter from backstage and sit in the front row of the audience: "I'm Tammy WhyNot and these are my *WhyNets*!" As she stands behind the microphone at center, she performs a country ballad called "Wrong Car in Memphis" about falling in love for the first time as her WhyNets perform backing vocals. Weaver's voice is shaky and often off-key, but this adds to the overall humor and relaxed nature of the piece. Tammy/Weaver states:

> And that is how Tammy WhyNot was born again—
> *again*! I saw a blinding light and knew I had to stop being
> a famous country western singer and start being a famous
> lesbian performance artist. And all because of the wrong
> car with the right girl in a parking lot in Memphis. (*What
> Tammy Needs to Know*)

Following this moment, the WhyNets take their seats as Tammy/Weaver continues: "When I started trying to be a famous lesbian performance artist, I realized there was a lot I needed to learn. So, I've been traveling all around the country to figure out what I need to know" (*What Tammy Needs to Know*). She jokes about what she needed to learn, such as feminist scholarship, Proust, civil rights, animal rights, modern philosophy, musical theory, and more sexual practices.

> But lately, I've been getting some funny feelings inside.
> Am I getting old? I feel something's not quite working
> right. I started to feel that I did not want to have sex as
> often. I didn't understand any of this, and so I started ask-
> ing some people, and so I decided what Tammy needs to
> know is about getting old and having sex. (*What Tammy
> Needs to Know*)

Weaver introduces her collaborators one by one and surveys her audience's age range. She asks the audience: "Are you still having sex?" Understandably, individual audience members are hesitant to answer, so she moves into the audience space to speak to individual people, asking the question again. The

Fig. 3.3 Lois Weaver as Tammy Whynot. Photo by Christa Holka. Courtesy Split Britches.

humorous banter she brings to this process as Tammy helps the audience relax and become more open about intimate matters, mirroring what she did pre-performance in the care homes. She asks audience members fill-in-the-blank questions, such as "When I think about age, I . . . " or "When I think about sex, I . . . " or "If I had a secret sex life, I . . . " Tammy then interviews the WhyNets with the same questions. Some speak about being in active sexual relationships while others discuss celibacy because of the loss of a partner. They also showcase individual talents, from mambo dancing to acapella ballads and poetry readings.

Instead of having a narrative through line like a realistic theatre production or dramatic work, the show is entirely based on audience response and the backstories of Tammy/Weaver's co-performers. The only pre-set aspects of the show are the songs, while everything else is loosely scripted and largely improvised by Tammy/Weaver as host. Another song in the show titled "Too Full to Finish" explicitly considers the types of regrets or hidden desires with regards to aging built out of Weaver's conversations with older people. She sings, "Too full to finish/but it's too good to leave/Well, I've got the grim reaper tugging on my sleeve/It's too full to finish, but it's too good to leave" (*What Tammy Needs to Know*). As with other numbers in the performance, the simple yet catchy lyrics are both effective and humorous, allowing audiences and the WhyNets to sing along as one would at a concert.

Near the end of the show, the WhyNets take center stage to answer a series of intimate questions about their sex lives. The answers range from experiences of being sexually active, to open relationships, to the subject of pleasure in general. Others talk about the longevity of their relationships, lovers who have died, and even sex toys. Discussing these desires out loud seems to be a very cathartic practice, not only for the WhyNets themselves, but also for the audiences who are also aging and thinking about shifting relationships to their bodies and to sex. (When I attended the performance in 2014, the WhyNets were extremely candid and remained remarkably unselfconscious about speaking these desires publicly, challenging social taboos about sex and aging at the center of Weaver's lesbian-feminist practice). In a section called "Broken Song," a video plays of Tammy getting ready in a dressing room (pre-filmed before the live performance). Before Tammy reenters the stage, she offers a monologue on age and aging, modeling her desire to challenge age stereotypes while also being open about her own vulnerabilities as a performer and in the persona:

> For more than 40 years, I've been standing behind this curtain, feeling my heart beatin' in my throat, floatin' between some kind of faintin' fit and a kind of heavy reality, a reality as heavy as this wig that I bought on Fourteenth Street. I don't know if this is incurable stage fright, or *age fright*! Standing here in the dark, in my golden autumn, thinking I'm not gonna be able to catch the tempo, sing the first syllable of the song, take the first step out of here without a stumble or a fall. (Weaver, *What Tammy Needs to Know*)

Tammy/Weaver's vulnerability and anxiety is calculated: she is displacing the audience's anxiety back onto herself, making

Tammy the vulnerable one and calling attention to her own exaggerated, parodic fictional performance as a lesbian performance artist modeled on a famous country singer.

The last song in the show is the most sexually evocative, titled "This Lemon's Still Got a Whole Lotta Juice." Weaver begins the song peeling a lemon with her hands and eats it painstakingly throughout the song, skin and all, as she is backed up on vocals by the WhyNets:

> 'Cause memories they can turn bitter
> And passion she can run dry
> Well this ol' fruit ain't no quitter
> Lemon can make a sweet meringue pie
> 'Cause lemons taste sweeter the older they get
> And without that tang! What's the use?
> It's not so bitter, this sweet yellow liquor
> This lemon's still got a whole lot of juice.
> (Weaver, What Tammy Needs to Know)

Fig. 3.4 Lois Weaver/Tammy WhyNot with her WhyNets, *What Tammy Needs to Know About Getting Old and Having Sex*, La MaMa, New York, 2015. Photo by Lori E. Seid. Courtesy of Split Britches.

As the performance ends, the metatheatrical premise becomes evident: we have been watching the warm-up and live sound-check for the concert, which is about to start. In the final moments, they cue up the first song again, "Sexy Back," as the lights fade to black.

CONCLUSION: TOO FULL TO FINISH

In the persona of Tammy, Weaver seeks to break down the barrier between audience and performer. As she stated in a recent interview,

> The line between Tammy and I has gotten thinner and thinner as I've aged . . . that's a gift of age. I think one thing that happened as I got older, amongst my peers and other people who are aging, is that we feel a little bit more *in* ourselves and a little *less* worried about the rough edges. (Weaver and Clark)

For decades, Weaver has thrived as a maker of feminist and queer performance, both as a solo artist and with Split Britches, in which a unique creative process has consistently helped articulate important critiques of the world through collaborative creation. This has been the case from early days at WOW with Split Britches all the way up to the present. Much less concerned about fixed aesthetics than about social and political engagement, her performances are informed by active desires and marginalized cultural reflections, seeing the potential to move beyond perceived limitations, especially for older artists and communities.

As a familiar stage persona, Tammy is a profound sounding board for Weaver's creative spirit—one which has only expanded with age, never settling for what seems easy or predictable. As Tammy, Weaver inspires audiences and collaborators, making them feel at home to share and create collectively as a good host always does. She consciously considers how, especially for older people, the past works effectively to enliven the present. The worlds that Weaver curates in *What Tammy Needs to Know About Getting Old and Having Sex* expand rather than decline with the energetic presence of her senior collaborators, incorporating her own aesthetic of lesbian-feminist performance-making that she has harnessed for decades to break apart the present as we think we know it in order to yield newer and *better* futures while acknowledging the real work it takes to get there. More than four decades into her career, she is still the community-driven, lesbian-feminist artist she was in the early days at WOW. Weaver has only gained more depth and insight with age as she continues to build new worlds and stronger bridges across generations of audiences and artists alike.

FURTHER RESOURCES

Davy, Kate. *Lady Dicks and Lesbian Brothers: Staging the Unimaginable at the WOW Café Theatre.* University of Michigan Press, 2011.
A detailed history of the development and legacy of the WOW Café Theatre.

Dolan, Jill, Holly Hughes, and Carmelita Tropicana, eds. *Memories of the Revolution: The First Ten Years of the WOW Café Theatre.* University of Michigan Press, 2015.
A collection of scripts, interviews, and commentary from foundational WOW Café Theatre artists.

Gillespie, Benjamin. "Lois Weaver." *The Routledge Anthology of Women's Theatre Theory and Dramatic Criticism.* Routledge, 2023, pp. 458–463.
A focused look at Lois Weaver's contributions to feminist and queer theatre and theory.

Weaver, Lois, and Jen Harvie, eds. *The Only Way Home is Through the Show: Performance Work of Lois Weaver.* Intellect Press, 2016.
The first book-length consideration of Weaver's career and work, including its history, aesthetics, inspirations, and impacts.

REFERENCES

Butler, Judith. *Gender Trouble: Feminism and the Subversion of Identity.* Routledge, 1990.

Case, Sue-Ellen. "Towards a Butch–Femme Aesthetic." *Feminist and Queer Performance: Critical Strategies.* Bloomsbury, 2009, pp. 31–48.

———. *Split Britches: Lesbian Practice/Feminist Performance.* Routledge, 1996.

Davy, Kate. "Reading Past the Heterosexual Imperative: *Dress Suits to Hire.*" *A Sourcebook on Feminist Theatre and Performance: On and Beyond the Stage*, ed. Carol Martin, Routledge, 1996, pp. 136–156.

Diamond, Elin. *Unmaking Mimesis: Essays on Feminism and Theatre.* Routledge, 1997.

Dolan, Jill. "The Dynamics of Desire: Sexuality and Gender in Pornography and Performance." *Theatre Journal,* vol. 39, no. 2, May 1987, pp. 156–174.

———. *The Feminist Spectator as Critic.* University of Michigan Press, 1988.

Split Britches. "About." http://www.split-britches.com/about. Accessed 15 August 2023.

———. "Tammy WhyNot." http://www.split-britches.com/tammywhynot-about-me. Accessed 16 August 2023.

Weaver, Lois. *What Tammy Needs to Know About Getting Old and Having Sex.* Unpublished manuscript, 2016.

Weaver, Lois, and Xandra Clark. "Queer Art Flashback Series with Lois Weaver and Xandra Clark," April 2020. https://vimeo.com/559039550/92335249a8. Accessed 15 August 2023.

CHAPTER 4

Harnessing the Political Power of Traditional Femininity in the 1980s

David Henry Hwang's *M. Butterfly* and Griselda Gambaro's *Antígona furiosa*

Rachel M. E. Wolfe

Across many times and cultures, people connect femininity, the feminine sphere, and "the feminine" with weakness. Common phrases, often associated with women, like "delicate flower," "damsel in distress," and "the weaker sex" show how widespread this idea is. Yet during the 1980s, popular feminist movements (and their associated art) became fascinated with the power of the traditionally "feminine": the female body, the home, and motherhood chief among them.[1] Coming on the heels of the "women's liberation" movements of the 1960s and 1970s—which were dominated by the concerns of white, middle-class women and largely centered around demanding the right to reject conventional femininity—the 1980s were a time when the global majority broke through the stranglehold that this niche group had held over the conversation. More feminists of color spoke about the particularities of the roles they had been forced into, how they differed from middle-class, first-world white women's experiences, and expressed that the new, intersectional feminism needed to take those experiences into account. The wholesale rejection of traditional femininity, in this moment, came to be seen as playing into the ideologies

DOI: 10.4324/9781003272854-5

of the patriarchy, which allocated women to certain roles and then devalued those roles because of women's perceived inferiority. To combat this ideology, scholarship, books, poems, films, and plays were written to reclaim and empower aspects of the human experience that had been devalued because of their associations with the idea of womanhood. Certain works, David Henry Hwang's *M. Butterfly* and Griselda Gambaro's *Antígona furiosa* among them, explored how the appearance of feminine "weakness" could be used to seize a public, political power that might otherwise be beyond reach. In these and other plays of the 1980s, conventional Western ideas about femininity are used by characters to gain power in spaces that are traditionally considered "masculine"— including the political sphere.

Written and performed in the 1980s, albeit in very different cultural contexts, David Henry Hwang's *M. Butterfly* (1988) and Griselda Gambaro's *Antígona furiosa* (1986) are touchstones in conversations about gender, power, and politics on the stage. Both adapt well-known historical plays that feature traditional gender roles, particularly around the domestic sphere and family relationships. Both refigure these previous plays in ways that politicize femininity and speak back to real-life political events. Yet they have their differences: Hwang's fusion-based approach to reconciling cultures, genders, and theatrical styles often viewed as opposites presents a stark contrast with Gambaro's tense, antagonistic pairings of those same things. In the sections below, we'll explore how these key theatre-makers and the different approaches of these plays trouble and reveal feminine "weakness" as a hidden source of political power.

FUSION: *M. BUTTERFLY,* ORIENTALISM, AND THE PERFORMANCE OF FEMININITY

In 1986, playwright David Henry Hwang saw a brief *New York Times* article about an espionage trial in France. Hwang found the article so inspirational that an excerpt from it serves as the playwright's notes on the first page of the play:

> A former French diplomat and a Chinese opera singer have been sentenced to six years in jail for spying for China after a two-day trial that traced a story of clandestine love and mistaken sexual identity. . . . Mr. Bouriscot was accused of passing information to China after he fell in love with Mr. Shi, whom he believed for twenty years to be a woman. *The New York Times*, May 11, 1986 (Hwang, 1989 n.p., ellipses in original)

Many people, including Hwang, wondered: "How could he not know?" (94–95). Bouriscot claimed that he had never seen Shi naked and he had not pressed because he believed modesty to be a Chinese custom (Bernstein 7). This detail sparked the idea for the play; as a Chinese-American, Hwang knew this was a mistaken assumption: there is no such Chinese custom (Hwang, 1989 94). However, there was another explanation for Bouriscot's 20-year mistake: **orientalism**.

Coined by Edward Said in 1978, "orientalism" refers to a Western/European fantasy of Asia as a place of luxury and pleasure, populated by people who are effeminate and eager to please. The term "orientalism" stems from outdated use of the term "oriental" to refer to anything from Asia, including people. Though "oriental" was still used in the 1980s—and in fact, is strategically used by Hwang in his play to refer to Western perceptions of Asians—today it is widely acknowledged as a limiting and insulting term, largely on account of its connection with justifications of Western colonial ambitions in Asia. Although "oriental" has been banned from federal documents in the United States and is frowned upon in general use, "orientalism"—referring to Western colonial attitudes, fantasies, and stereotypes about Asia and Asians—is still used to critique that particular set of ideas. Orientalism, in a nutshell, is the idea that Asia exists to serve the West and is a playground that Westerners use at their pleasure, whether that be colonial, sexual, hedonistic, or some combination of all three. Though Said wrote specifically about Western depictions of the Middle East, many of the tenets he used to define orientalism align with Western depictions of East Asia. Particularly interesting to Hwang was the orientalist depiction of Asian women as "demure and submissive" (94) and sexually available to masculine Western men.

This fanciful vision of Asian women was sometimes referred to by the term "Butterfly," a reference to Italian composer Giaccomo Puccini's opera *Madama Butterfly*. In Hwang's circles, "speaking of an Asian woman, we would sometimes say, 'She's pulling a Butterfly,' which meant playing the submissive Oriental number" (Hwang, 1989 95). Essentially, to "pull a Butterfly" is to play into Western misconceptions of the East by assuming a fake persona and using stereotypes to one's own advantage. Although an Italian opera, Puccini's *Madama Butterfly* is set in Japan and centers around the marriage between a Japanese woman, Cio-Cio-san (a.k.a. "Madame Butterfly") and an American sailor, Pinkerton. The most famous of numerous adaptations stretching back to Pierre Loti's novel *Madame Chrysanthéme* (1887), *Madama Butterfly* depicts the marriage in a stereotypically orientalist way: the Eastern woman is devoted to her Western husband despite the fact he treats her badly and abandons her. When Pinkerton finally returns—with a new, American wife—Madame Butterfly commits suicide (Puccini 268). Hwang calls out the orientalism in this plot, describing it as "yet another lotus blossom pining away for a cruel Caucasian man, and dying for her love" (Hwang, 1989 95). As a story about a Japanese character, set in Japan, yet written by an Italian using the conventions of Western opera, playing into Western fantasies of the East, and nearly always starring a Western diva,[2] *Madama Butterfly* not only ticks all the geographic boxes for orientalist Western fantasy but also all the gendered ones: Butterfly is helpless in the face of Pinkerton's masculinity and supposed cultural superiority, choosing him over a Japanese suitor and abandoning her religion and clothing styles in favor of Pinkerton's.

Inspired by this image of Butterfly, orientalism, and questions around Bouriscot's motives, Hwang's "deconstructivist *Madame Butterfly*" was born (95). A mash-up of his own fictionalized version of the real-life espionage case and his adaptation/mockery of Puccini's opera, he created the ambiguously titled *M. Butterfly*. "M." is the French abbreviation for "*monsieur*" and therefore equivalent to "Mr." without being too obvious for an English-speaking audience. Widely regarded as Hwang's masterpiece, *M. Butterfly* won the Tony Award for best play in 1988 and was a Pulitzer Prize finalist in 1989. It also enjoyed a Broadway revival in 2017, for which Hwang revised the script to incorporate new information about the real-life espionage case and explore updated understandings of gender and gender fluidity. The play combines the staging conventions and music of both Western and Chinese opera, weaving together reality, orientalist fantasy, and well-known fiction. In it, Bouriscot metamorphosizes into Rene Gallimard, the French diplomat who envisions himself into the role of Pinkerton in the excerpts from and commentaries on *Madama Butterfly* sprinkled throughout the play. Shi becomes the musically named Song Liling, a spy for China's revolutionary government and a male *dan*.

What is a *dan*? In Chinese opera, all characters are sorted into one of four "role-types": *sheng* roles (male characters), *jing* roles (painted-face characters[3]), *chou* roles (clown characters), and *dan* roles (female characters). Traditionally, actor-singer-acrobats who perform in Chinese opera are trained from the beginning to play one role-type, which they play their entire careers. While both men and women play *dan* roles, men have most commonly played *dan* roles since Emperor Quianlong banned actresses from the stage by royal decree in 1772. Although the ban was lifted in 1923, a century of all-male acting troupes firmly established a tradition of male actors playing female characters on the stage. Moreover, the hottest global superstar of Chinese opera was a male *dan*: Mei Lanfang. Beginning in 1904 and for nearly 40 years, Mei Lanfang toured the world, introducing foreign audiences to Chinese opera. He remains *the* face of Chinese opera within and outside of China, even decades after his death in 1961. His performances inspired numerous figures in Western theatre, most notably Bertolt Brecht, who based the concept of *Verfremdungseffekt*, or "the alienation effect," on his encounter with Chinese opera during one of Mei Lanfang's performances (Tian 44–45). Perhaps unsurprisingly, the cross-dressing of Mei's performances as a male *dan* sparked much interest and commentary in the West (see Goldstein).

The character Song Liling in *M. Butterfly* is a fusion of multiple people, both historical and fictional. Most obviously the fictionalized version of the real-life Chinese spy Shi, Song also plays Butterfly in the sections of Puccini's opera that appear in the play and, as a male *dan*, Song reflects Mei Lanfang. For example, in the original version of *M. Butterfly*, Song asks Gallimard to attend her/his performance in *The Drunken Beauty*, one of Mei Lanfang's signature roles, which survives on film to this day (Hwang, 1989 26, Chen et al.). In the updated script for the 2017 revival, this role was replaced with *Madame White Snake*, also famously performed by Mei Lanfang (Hwang, 2017 25). Chameleon-like, Song Liling's character shifts throughout the play. Gallimard and audiences alike are taken in first by Song's performances in both Western and Chinese opera, then by the offstage performance as Gallimard's "Perfect Woman," a term capitalized in the text to describe the idealized version of Song he fell in love with. It is further evident in the different personas Song adopts in the presence of the Revolutionary Guards and the French court system. Even the pronouns in the script reflect Song's fluidity: at different points in the play (both the original and updated versions), Song is referred to in the stage directions using either she/her/hers or he/him/his pronouns. Song (and the actor playing the role) assumes whatever postures, words, gender presentation, or character is required by the present situation, to the point that it becomes virtually impossible to tell when (or if) Song is acting.

In effect, Song "pulls a Butterfly" multiple times and in multiple ways, but the most important is Song's metaphorical Butterfly performance as Gallimard's "Perfect Woman," his Western orientalist fantasy. In order to play Gallimard's "Perfect Woman," Song adopts an air of timidity, flatters all things Western, and puts down her/his own culture—much like the less ironic Cio-Cio-san from *Madama Butterfly*. The first time (s)he invites Gallimard home, Song puts on a performance of being ashamed about having issued the invitation:

> Hard as I try to be modern, to speak like a man, to hold a Western woman's strong face up to my own . . .in the end, I fail. A small, frightened heart beats too quickly and

Fig. 4.1 Lucas Verbrugghe and Jake Manabat in the 2019 production by South Coast Repertory (Costa Mesa, CA) of *M. Butterfly* by David Henry Hwang. Photo by Jordan Kubat/SCR.

> gives me away. Monsieur Gallimard, I'm a Chinese girl. I've never . . . never invited a man up to my flat before. The forwardness of my actions makes my skin burn. (Hwang, 1989 30–31)

Song builds up men and Westerners while putting her-/himself down and uses a stereotypically feminine tactic: appearing weak, frightened, and inexperienced—a damsel in distress. Gallimard, in turn, revels in his (perceived) power, keeping Song waiting for two months before initiating their sexual relationship (31–41). Once established, Song deploys these same feminine, orientalist tactics to gain classified information: self-effacement, downplaying Chinese culture, uplifting the West, and amplifying Gallimard's masculinity. Again, it works: Gallimard discloses state secrets to Song, who passes them on to the government (47–48). Later, when (s)he feels Gallimard slipping away, Song plays the ultimate feminine card: motherhood. (S)he announces (s)he is pregnant (59–61), disappears to the country for several months (66), procures a baby via the Revolutionary government (61–62), and tells

Gallimard it is their son (66–67). Through performance, this "Perfect Woman," the epitome of femininity, becomes real.

In contrast, Comrade Chin, Song's contact in the Chinese Revolutionary Guard to whom (s)he reports what (s)he has learned by spying on Gallimard, is a woman who is addressed by the gender-neutral title "comrade," dresses in a unisex Mao suit, occupies a position of political authority (a traditionally masculine social position), and explicitly mocks Song's feminine garb (48). As a female-bodied person who performs masculinity and has overt political power, [4] Chin is a foil to Song, a male-bodied person who performs femininity to gain covert political power. Taken together, these two characters show that "femininity" has nothing to do with bodies: femininity may as easily be rejected and shed by a female-bodied person as it can be embraced and acquired by a male-bodied one. One of Song's most telling lines is delivered to Comrade Chin:

SONG. Miss Chin? Why, in the Peking Opera, are women's roles played by men?

CHIN. I don't know. Maybe, a reactionary remnant of male—

SONG. No. (*Beat*) Because only a man knows how a woman is supposed to act. (63)

Song claims that femininity itself is a patriarchal invention, in the same way that the "submissive oriental" is a Western invention.

These inventions and fantasies, fusing gender and national origin into a feminized East and masculinized West, are key to Song's power over Gallimard. In the court scene, Song explains:

The West thinks of itself as masculine [. . .] so the East is feminine—weak, delicate, poor [. . .] You expect Oriental countries to submit to your guns, and you expect Oriental women to be submissive to your men. [. . .] When [Gallimard] finally met his fantasy woman, he wanted

> more than anything to believe that she was, in fact, a woman. And second, I am an Oriental. And being an Oriental, I could never be completely a man. (83)

This last phrase, possibly the best known from M. *Butterfly*, is the strongest critique of orientalism in the play. In orientalism, the world is understood in terms of mutually exclusive opposites—East–West, male–female, dominant–submissive, familiar–foreign. Gallimard is blinded by this cultural fantasy, and Song plays into that fantasy to keep Gallimard from noticing the spying, the political intrigue, and his/her sex. Butterfly, the fanciful creation of Western minds and bias, is just as fictional as the fanciful creations that form *dan* roles: a type of femininity invented for the stage and performed by men because "only a man knows how a woman is supposed to act."

Throughout M. *Butterfly*, Hwang blurs boundaries and mocks binaristic thinking. East and West, male and female, fantasy and reality, Western and Chinese opera, and past and present become so blended, fused, and *con*fused that disentangling them becomes impossible. Performance is all: what are we performing and for whom? What power can be seized by playing into which fantasies? In Hwang's hands, femininity is revealed as fiction that can be performed at will. If you appear weak in the process, who cares? In the end, you're still the one holding the state secrets.

OPPOSITION: *ANTÍGONA FURIOSA*, ARGENTINA'S DIRTY WAR, AND THE DOUBLE BIND OF FEMININITY

If Hwang's play proves femininity to be a fiction, Gambaro's reveals it as a fiction that is impossible to maintain. Premiering in 1986 in the wake of the Dirty War in Argentina, Griselda Gambaro's *Antígona furiosa* dramatizes the double bind of femininity that the Madres of the Plaza de Mayo found themselves in during the war. Caught between a mother's duty to care for family and the woman's place in the home, many women were unable to reconcile both demands of femininity in a world where fighting patriarchal authority in the public, political sphere was the only way to care for family.

Unlike most wars, Argentina's Dirty War was not fought between two nations; rather it was a secret war the military *junta,* Argentina's government from 1976 to 1983, waged against its own people. Individuals the government suspected of having communist sympathies frequently "disappeared," which is to say they were secretly abducted, tortured for information, murdered, and quietly disposed of, without the government informing anyone what had happened to them.[5] Moreover, official records of *los desaparecidos,* the people who disappeared, were destroyed, so that when relatives and friends asked after them, they were told no such person existed. The secrecy around these abductions and murders created a quiet terror in which large swaths of the population did not know—or were unwilling to openly acknowledge—that anything was wrong.

The abductions were revealed on a very public stage beginning in 1977 with a protest on the Plaza de Mayo, the space in front of the presidential palace in Buenos Aires, by the Madres, a group of mothers whose sons and daughters had disappeared and whose attempts to find them had met a bureaucratic stone wall of erased records.[6] As they searched, 14 mothers found each other, realized that the disappearances were widespread, and organized the first public protest. This protest, which drew no official response from the government, became a repeated act and the group became known as *Madres de la Plaza de Mayo* (Mothers of the Plaza de Mayo). Every Thursday at 3:30 pm, the group met and walked in circles around the plaza, often in pairs to avoid the law against public meetings of groups of three or more.[7] Most held photographs of their missing children, and the practice of wearing white kerchiefs on their heads—often embroidered with missing children's names and birthdates—became a recognizable symbol. As word of their protests spread, more mothers of the disappeared arrived, publicly, visibly demanding the return of their missing children. *"Aparición con vida"* ("back alive") became their rallying cry, quickly drawing international attention from global human rights organizations and prompting calls for a UN investigation into human rights abuses in Argentina.

Though they did not personally topple the regime, the Madres successfully drew attention to these horrific crimes and inspired action to find and identify the remains of the disappeared after the regime fell. Thanks to their efforts, families could properly mourn and bury their loved ones. DNA testing that they instigated revealed that three of the original Madres were themselves disappeared in retaliation for beginning the protests (McDonnell; Goni). Though far short of *aparición con vida*, these measures have helped undo the campaign of widespread gaslighting under the previous regime, which maintained that these women's children never existed and referred to the mothers as *"las locas"* ("the crazy women") (Taylor 229).

Griselda Gambaro has made an entire career out of drawing attention and visibility to the human rights abuses that have taken place in Argentina. From early works like *El Campo* (*The Camp*, 1967), which drew attention to the growth of fascism in Argentina and predicted the violence to come, to works like *Antígona furiosa* that premiered after the war and reflected on its enduring psychological scars, Gambaro's plays and novels focus on the culpability of those who do not speak up, those who do not resist, and those whose willingness to ignore violence allows it to continue. Her novel *Ganarse la muerte*, written during the dictatorship of the military *junta*, was officially banned by the regime, an act that caused Gambaro to flee to Spain. During this time, without an Argentine audience for her work, Gambaro ceased writing plays, only resuming after the fall of the *junta* and her return to Argentina. *Antígona furiosa* was one of these homecoming works, a look back at the Dirty War, *los desaparecidos*, the Madres of the Plaza de Mayo, and the silent majority who stood by and let it happen.

Like *M. Butterfly*, *Antígona furiosa* is a deconstructed adaptation of an earlier work: *Antigone* by Sophocles. Also like

M. Butterfly, it utilizes many references to make its points: Antígona's first lines are from *Hamlet* and the play's title is a reference to *Orlando Furioso*, a Renaissance epic about a knight who is driven mad by love.[8] Unlike *M. Butterfly*, the oppositions raised in *Antígona furiosa* do not blur into one another. Starkly divided and antagonistic, *Antígona furiosa* presents an irreconcilable clash between ancient and modern, dead and alive, tragedy and comedy, woman and men, love and hate, the disappeared and the callously indifferent.

Gambaro's version of *Antigone* has only three characters: the ancient and already deceased title character (Antígona) and two modern male figures with ancient names, Corifeo (Coryphaeus, or "leader of the chorus") and Antinoo (Antinous, "against reason"). This chorus of two exists to stand outside of Antígona's reality, mock her pain, and purposefully misunderstand her. Occupying a space that looks like an Argentine street café, they make fun of Antígona for not knowing what coffee is and devolve from there (Gambaro, *Antígona* 197–198). A fourth "character" appears in the form of an elaborate prop: Creonte (Creon), arguably the main character in Sophocles' *Antigone*, is played in Gambaro's adaptation by "*Una carcasa* [. . .] *Cuando el Corifeo se introduce en ella, assume obviamente el trono y el poder*" (196; "A shell [. . .] When Choryphaeus goes into it, he obviously assumes the throne and power," my trans.). As a device, Creonte becomes a stand-in for the military *junta*. He is an empty symbol of power and dominance, whose will may be carried out by anyone who can mold themselves into his shape.

In these characters, Gambaro sets up several oppositional pairs: ancient vs. modern, woman vs. men, human vs. hollow symbol. As Diana Taylor describes it, there are also opposite genres in play: "Antígona seems to exist on a separate, distant, 'tragic' plane [. . .] The other two characters occupy the roles of contemporary spectators watching Antígona's ordeal" (212). While Antígona is in a tragedy, the chorus of buffoons act as though they are witnessing a comedy. In ancient Greek plays, the chorus served as an onstage representative for the audience. In Gambaro's chorus, their disconnect from the main character in both time and genre presents a jarring clash

Fig. 4.2 Hal Cohen, Adam Ferguson, and April Singley in *Antígona furiosa*, directed by Lila Rachel Becker. This production pays homage to the pyramidal cage through the rope's placement. Photo by Todd Brian Backus.

that is never reconciled. These opposites are reinforced by the visuals: in the first production of *Antígona furiosa*, the set designer separated the ancient, tragic plane from the modern, comedic one by trapping Antígona in a "pyramidal cage" for the whole performance—a design convention that has become a well-known part of the play, while not prescribed in the script (see Taylor 253–257; Feitlowitz 135; Figure 4.2 above). The association of pyramids with the ancient world marks Antígona as an ancient figure, permanently separated from the modern Argentina that forms the rest of the set. Moreover, pyramids are temples to death: elaborate tombs built by the powerful on the backs—and deaths—of the powerless. Combined with the opening image of Antígona already hanged (Gambaro 197), the pyramid makes Antígona a representative of death, permanently separated from the life around her.

More oppositional pairs emerge when we consider *Antígona furiosa* as an adaptation. Sophocles' *Antigone* is a widely known play about the clash of opposing, irreconcilable forces.

In Sophocles, Creon, king of Thebes, made a declaration about his predecessor kings, who had killed each other over the throne. Creon decreed that the one who had attacked the city would remain unburied, a feast for crows and dogs (an act of deep disrespect in ancient Greece[9]), while the one who had defended the city would be buried with all honors (lines 215–231). Antigone, sister to both deceased kings, fulfills her religious (and feminine) duty to properly mourn her dead relatives by burying the brother who had been left out as carrion, defying Creon's order (lines 436–492). Sophocles's *Antigone* is a struggle between the public, masculine sphere of the *polis* (city), which must punish those who break its laws, and the private, feminine sphere of the *oikos* (household), where family obligations reign supreme.

What happens when the *polis* threatens the *oikos*? How can a woman, tasked with keeping out of politics and caring for the family at home, respond in an appropriately feminine way when politics kills her family? She cannot both avoid the public sphere *and* care for family; she becomes political in defying the state, even as she does the traditionally feminine care work of burial and mourning. This is the double bind of traditional femininity that links Antigone and the Madres of the Plaza de Mayo: the keepers of the *oikos* must venture into the *polis* after their missing male relatives.

The gendered associations of what women do in public, in both the ancient Greek and modern Argentinian versions of the story, are pointed. In ancient Greece, mourning, burial, and death rites were women's work, and represented a feminine power which was considered so strong that excessive funeral rites were banned under the Solonic Laws in Athens (Reitzammer 24). In modern Argentina, the specifically feminine displays of public grief by the Madres were strategic: mothers marched, mothers protested, mothers demanded their children back alive—not fathers. If these women had been joined in public grief by their male partners, the protests would have been viewed as an attack on the government. A protest by men would have been violently stopped, and that violence would have been seen as justifiable defense. A protest by women, especially women who made a display of traditional femininity as the Madres did by wearing kerchiefs and house slippers (Taylor 235–236) and rooting their calls for justice firmly in mother-love, could be dismissed or quietly suppressed through more disappearances. To openly retaliate against a group as "weak" and "feminine" as mothers would have damaged public perception of the *junta* in a way that violent suppression of male protest never could.

Gambaro's version of *Antigone*, written for a modern Argentinian audience familiar with the Madres' protests and the ancient Greek play, uses these gender politics to create a version of Antígona whose power is in her grief, her weakness, and her femininity. Antígona mourns; trapped in her own private temple to death, she revives herself at the beginning of the play only to "camina[r] entre sus muertos, en una extraña marcha donde se cae y se incorpora, cae y se incorpora" (Gambaro 200; "[walk] among her dead, a strange march in which she falls and gets up, falls and gets up", my trans.), a circular walk of mourning that conjures the Madres' circular progress around the plaza. Antígona weeps over the empty shroud that represents the body of her unburied brother (201), a clear reference to the bodiless mourning undertaken by relatives of *los desaparecidos*. Most importantly, she maintains repeatedly that "Porque soy mujer, nací, para compartir el amor y no el odio" (204 and 217; "Because I am a woman, I was born to share love and not hate," my trans.). Antígona is motivated by love, only getting involved in politics to fulfill the dictates of love (burying her brother) and wishing she could abandon the hate that marks the masculine political sphere and causes death. In the end, though, Antígona voices her final lament: "el odio manda. *(Furiosa)* ¡El resto es silencio! *(Se da muerte. Con furia)*" (217; "hate commands. *(Furious)* The rest is silence! *(She kills herself. With fury)*," my trans.). Beginning in death and returning to death at the end, Gambaro's Antígona is immersed in the feminine act of mourning, showing love for her dead brother. Her defiance of Creon is an afterthought, an incidental result of *his* actions, not hers.

In both Sophocles and Gambaro's work, Creon/Creonte drives Antigone/Antígona to her death. As punishment for breaking the law, he entombs Antigone/Antígona in a cave with one day's supply of food (Sophocles lines 870–878; Gambaro 211). Like the three Madres who joined the *desaparecidos*, Antígona is the loving, feminine family member of an "enemy of the state" whose public display of mourning was viewed as so threatening that she was killed in turn. But like the collective Madres who return, week after week, to march in the Plaza de Mayo, she cannot be silenced. As she returned from death at the beginning of the play, so she will return again: "Aun quiero enterrar a Polinices. 'Siempre' querré enterrar a Polinices. Aunque nazca mil veces y él muera mil veces" (Gambaro 217; "I still want to bury Polynices. I will 'always' want to bury Polynices. Even if I were to be born a thousand times, and he were to die a thousand times," my trans.). This line, uttered toward the end of the play and between Antígona's two deaths, carries a special resonance for "siempre" ("always") and the repetition of the story implied in "mil veces" ("a thousand times"). Having seen her come from death and return to death, we know she will resurrect again, make the same choices, and die again. As a figure whose story has been adapted "a thousand times," Antígona's pronouncement rings true: in all adaptations, in every performance, she will always want to bury her brother, in the same way that, with every march around the Plaza de Mayo, the Madres want their children "back alive." There is power in this grief, in the loving and feminine work of mourning, in Antígona's (and the Madres') weakness. This power commands attention and withstands the dismissive mockery of the men outside the cage—or the plaza.

THE 1980S: A MILESTONE IN STAGING FEMININITY

In *M. Butterfly* and *Antígona furiosa*, central characters adopt types of traditional femininity that appear weak but directly translate to power in the political realm. In *M. Butterfly*, it is the power of invisibility, the power of the chameleon and the spy: the power to go unnoticed, and consequently, to learn powerful secrets. In *Antígona furiosa*, it is the power of visibility, the power to revive the dead, and the power to uncover secrets. While *M. Butterfly* blurs, confuses, and crosses boundaries, *Antígona furiosa* sheds light on the irreconcilable, on oppositions that can never be resolved. Yet in both, leaning into traditional femininity, caregiver roles, and vulnerability is a step toward claiming power in the masculinized political realm.

The late 1980s were a moment when women's fiction, women's theatre, and the feminist movement often concerned themselves with reclaiming and validating the traditional feminine sphere. In complex ways that reflect the different political realities surrounding their creation, Hwang's and Gambaro's works share and explore this concern. Whether in the form of East–West fusion or antagonistic opposition, whether the person employing (and deploying) femininity is male or female, these plays investigate how catering to a traditional view of femininity and "the feminine" may translate into political power despite—or even because of—the common assumption that femininity is weakness. This paradox forms the crux of both plays, and provides another lens on staging genders, particularly in feminist playwriting of the 1980s.

FURTHER RESOURCES

Bautista Gutiérrez, Gloria. *Voces femeninas de Hispanoamérica: antología*. University of Pittsburgh Press, 1996.
This Spanish-language anthology of women's writing from Latin America places Griselda Gambaro in the context of other Latina writers working in a variety of genres.

Moraga, Cherríe, and Gloria Anzaldúa, eds. *This Bridge Called My Back: Writings by Radical Women of Color*. Persephone Press, 1981.
This key collection from feminist writers of color in the early 1980s combines scholarship with poetry, personal narrative, and other types of artistic writing to paint a diverse picture of feminism.

Tian, Min. "Male *Dan*: The Paradox of Sex, Acting, and Perception of Female Impersonation in Traditional Chinese Theatre." *Asian Theatre Journal*, vol. 17, no. 1, 2000, pp. 78–97.
A brief but thorough look at the history of men acting women's roles in Chinese theatre, including perceptions of the practice from Chinese and foreign (Japanese and Western) perspectives.

REFERENCES

Ariosto, Lodovico. *Orlando Furioso: A New Verse Translation.* Trans. David R. Slavitt. Belknap Press of Harvard University Press, 2009.

Bernstein, Richard. "France Jails 2 in Odd Case of Espionage." *The New York Times*, May 11, 1986. https://www.nytimes.com/1986/05/11/world/france-jails-2-in-odd-case-of-espionage.html. Accessed December 30, 2023.

Bonds, Alexandra B. *Beijing Opera Costumes: The Visual Communication of Character and Culture.* University of Hawai'i Press, 2008.

Boyd, Melinda. "'Re-Orienting' the Vision: Ethnicity and Authenticity from Suzuki to Comrade Chin." *A Vision of the Orient: Texts, Intertexts, and Contexts of Madame Butterfly*, ed. Jonathan Wisenthal, Sherrill E. Grace, Melinda Boyd, Brian McIlroy, and Vera Micznik. University of Toronto Press, 2006.

Chen, Mei-Juin, Lisa Muskat, Jian Shi, Bronwyn Barkan, Ross Blaufarb, Lanfang Mei, Syou-Ling Fu, et al. *The Worlds of Mei Lanfang*. Lotus Films, 2005.

Feitlowitz, Marguerite. "Griselda Gambaro." *BOMB*, no. 32, July 1, 1990, https://bombmagazine.org/articles/griselda-gambaro. Accessed December 30, 2023.

———. "Translator's Note." In *Information for Foreigners: Three Plays by Griselda Gambaro*. Northwestern University Press, 1992.

Gambaro, Griselda. "*Antígona furiosa.*" In *Griselda Gambaro: Teatro 3*, 5th ed. Ediciones de la Flor, 2003.

———. "*El Campo.*" In *Griselda Gambaro: Teatro 1*. Ediciones de la Flor, 1984.

———. *Ganarse la muerte*. El Cuenco De Plata, 2016.

Goldstein, Joshua. "Mei Lanfang and the Nationalization of Peking Opera, 1912–1930." *Positions*, vol. 7, no. 2, 1999, pp. 377–420.

Goni, Uki. "Pope Francis and the Missing Marxist." *The Guardian*, December 11, 2013, https://www.theguardian.com/world/2013/dec/11/pope-francis-argentina-esther-careaga. Accessed December 30, 2023.

Honig, Emily. "Maoist Mappings of Gender: Reassessing the Red Guards." In *Chinese Femininities, Chinese Masculinities: A Reader*, ed. Susan Brownell and Jeffrey N. Wasserstrom. University of California Press, 2002, pp. 255–268.

Howe, Sara Eleanor. "The Madres de la plaza de mayo: asserting motherhood; rejecting feminism?" *Journal of International Women's Studies*, vol. 7, no. 3, March 2006, pp. 43–50.

Hwang, David Henry. *M. Butterfly.* Plume, 1989.

———. *M. Butterfly: Broadway Tie-In Edition.* Plume, 2017.

Lewis, Paul H. *Guerrillas and Generals: The "Dirty War" in Argentina.* Praeger Publishers, 2002.

McDonnell, Patrick J. "Argentines Remember a Mother Who Joined the 'Disappeared'." *Los Angeles Times*, March 24, 2006. https://www.latimes.com/archives/la-xpm-2006-mar-24-fg-dirtywar24-story.html. Accessed December 30, 2023.

Mystakidou, Kyriaki, Eleni Tsilika, Efi Parpa, Emmanuela Katsouda, and Lambros Vlahos. "Death and Grief in the Greek Culture." *Omega*, vol. 50, no. 1, 2005, pp. 23–34.

Puccini, Giacomo. *Madama Butterfly. Puccini's Operas: Libretti in Italian/English.* Trans. Burton D. Fisher. Opera Journeys Publishing, 2003.

Reitzammer, Laurialan. *The Athenian Adonia in Context: The Adonis Festival as Cultural Practice.* University of Wisconsin Press, 2016.

Said, Edward. *Orientalism.* Vintage Books, 1979.

Shakespeare, William. *Hamlet.* Floating Press, 2008.

Sophocles. *Antigone.* In *Antigone. The Women of Trachis. Philoctetes. Oedipus at Colonus,* ed. and trans. Hugh Lloyd-Jones. Loeb Classical Library 21. Harvard University Press, 1994.

Taylor, Diana. "Trapped in Bad Scripts: The Mothers of the Plaza de Mayo." In *Disappearing Acts: Spectacles of Gender and Nationalism in Argentina's 'Dirty War.'* Duke University Press, 1997, pp. 224–269.

Tian, Min. *Poetics of Difference and Displacement: Twentieth-Century Chinese-Western Intercultural Theatre.* Hong Kong University Press, 2008.

NOTES

1 I use "traditional" to mean rooted in longstanding and widely accepted cultural ideas. While the specifics of traditional femininity shift between traditions and among cultures, I am referring here generally to the ways that tradition plays into longstanding cultural ideation.

2 Melinda Boyd explored how a Japanese singer performing the role in 1915 reified Western expectations that it is more "properly" done by white singers in yellowface (69–70).

3 Support characters for the main storyline, *jing* personalities and social positions are expressed through symbolic face paint. See Bonds on the expression of role-types through costuming and makeup.

4 Under the Chinese communist regime, attitudes were that gender, like all social categories besides class, served as a strategy of the rich (bourgeoise) to keep the poor (proletariat) fighting among themselves rather than uniting against the bourgeoise. Thus, the communist party introduced unisex dress codes to remove social distinctions between men and women, allowed

women into positions of power, and professed to give women equal social standing with men. See Honig.

5 For a complete history of the Dirty War, see Lewis.

6 For a more about the Madres, see Howe.

7 On the specific tactics and practices of the Madres, see Taylor.

8 See Ariosto for an English translation of this epic poem.

9 Burial in ancient Greek contexts had implications for the next phase of the dead person's existence. People who did not receive proper burial could not cross the river Styx and enter the afterlife; they were stuck in limbo. On Greek death and burial, see Mystakidou et al.

CHAPTER 5

Staging Genders and Centering Women's Voices in West African Theatres

Heather Jeanne Denyer and Ngozi Udengwu

In her 2013 book *Africana Women Writers: Performing Diaspora, Staging Healing,* DeLinda Marzette explains how "in an attempt to transgress hegemonic boundaries, resisting Africana women writers recreate, redefine, and renegotiate a space to thrive on their own terms" (11). This chapter examines two resistant West African women playwrights who altered the shape of theatre in the late 20th century: Werewere Liking and Tess Onwueme. By shifting the focus of theatre to women in society, rewriting histories and myths to include women, and reimagining the way that stories are told on stage, their groundbreaking work opened new spaces for women in the male-dominated fields of literature and performance, where they reappropriated traditional practices to define new possibilities. Because of the legacies of these women theatre-makers, there are many more women writing for and performing in West African theatres today.

Theatres in West Africa can be divided in linguistic terms as well as by genre and intended audiences. The performance traditions featured in these theatres have existed for centuries and are often particular to local groups and performed in one of the nearly 2,000 African languages. Jaliya (or Griot performance) and Sogo bò puppetry performance—both of which are discussed in this chapter—are two such traditions. Of course, histories of colonization impacted perceptions and types of West African theatre. During the Berlin Conference in 1884–1885, European powers carved up the African continent

DOI: 10.4324/9781003272854-6

to divide and reap the resources for the benefit of European countries and to control the people. The imposition of French and English educational systems in the colonized territories influenced how written plays developed in the 20th century in each country. While multiple chapters could be written about the theatre and approaches to staging genders that emerged in different countries across the African continent, this chapter focuses on two countries: Ivory Coast and Nigeria. In Ivory Coast, theatre and performance was influenced by historical French theatre, written in Alexandrins (12 syllable verse lines), from Molière, Corneille, and Racine, in the early 20th century and by absurdist writers like Eugène Ionesco and Jean Genet in more contemporary work. For Nigeria and Ghana, there was a strong emphasis on Shakespeare as a model, particularly prior to and in the early years of African states' independence during the 1960s.

During the 1960s–1980s, many African nations gained independence from colonizers, and during that time, common themes emerged in theatre, including African heroes and legends, myths, and histories. In the 1990s to today, social realities like migration, generational differences, postcolonial identities and oppression, and, increasingly, women's place in society have become the focus of many theatrical works and published plays. This last theme, gender and women's place in society is the focus of this chapter. This topic became increasingly prominent in the 1990s with the inclusion of more women in theatre-making. During this time, more women pursued university education and became involved in academic theatre. Simultaneously, more professional theatre companies formed which included women performers, and eventually, directors. More women also began to write plays. While many have heard of the great Ghanaian playwright, Ama Ata Aidoo (1942–2023), the first published woman playwright in the West African region with her 1965 play *The Dilemma of a Ghost,* there are many more women writing for the stages of West Africa whose work carved the path for current and next generations of women theatre-makers.

This chapter is divided into two parts and cowritten by a Nigerian scholar of Anglophone theatres and a US scholar focused on Francophone theatres. The first part considers Werewere Liking, who is based in Ivory Coast, and her plays *The Power of Um* and *Sogolon*. The second explores Tess Onwueme of Nigeria and her plays *The Broken Calabash* and *The Reign of Wazobia*. By centering the voices of two West African women artists and their plays, the chapter demonstrates how these leading theatre makers stake their claim for a voice and visibility in the public sphere and how they defy gender conventions to redefine how women are represented and gender is staged in contemporary African theatres.

WEREWERE LIKING

Werewere Liking was raised in Cameroon and initiated into Bassa ritual practices by her paternal grandparents. (The Bassa are one of the hundreds of West African ethnic groups, each with language and rituals unique to the group.) A self-taught writer, she moved to Abidjan, Ivory Coast, where she established her own artist community called Ki-Yi Mbock—a Bassa term that means the ultimate knowledge of the universe. She was one of few women artists to train with artist Yaya Coulibaly in Mali in traditional Sogo bò puppetry techniques in 1977, and in 1982 she was one of the first West African theatre-makers to present work at the annual French-language theatre festival in Limoges, France. She continues to not only develop young artists but also create tradition-infused performances. These performances begin and end with a ritual called Hijingo, wherein the performers dance in circles in every corner of the stage and initiate a traditional call and response for all participants to recognize the spirits being honored. They also incorporate dances and music from other African groups such as the Wolof and Masai and often utilize puppetry. In this way, students training at Ki-Yi and audiences who experience their work are engaged in the rich cultural practices that have long been used in storytelling in Africa, while also witnessing plays and productions that speak to contemporary concerns for Africans, and often, in particular, concerns for women. As Liking explained in our 2017 personal interview, "I lean more towards the problems [of women] and the responsible and positive reaction of

Fig. 5.1 Werewere Liking at Ki-Yi MBock Villa, Abidjan, Côte d'Ivoire, 2017. Photo by Heather Denyer.

women to them, in the perpetuation of life, in its improvement, and in evolution."

Part of Liking's efforts through theatre and educational work at Ki-Yi Mbock includes promoting women. She believes that "to build up a man is good; to build up a woman is to build up ten men" (quoted in Mielly, her translation). In many of her plays, including *The Power of Um* and *Sogolon*, she re-centers women in African histories and infuses older traditions with new uses to build up younger generations.

The Power of Um

Written in 1979, *The Power of Um* (*La puissance d'Um* in the original French and Bassa) centers on the titular Bassa female deity who signifies fertility, purity, and peace as well as music, dance, and theatre. Thus, the performance ritual—both the actual Hijingo and the full play as ritual drama—serves the audience as a community in parallel to the ritual that heals the community in the play. The play's last words—"May the Power of Um descend upon us!" (Liking 60)—call upon the deity Um, and many aspects of the performance convey ritual elements to heighten the experience of all participants. The audience seating consists of rocks, benches, and logs, each covered with a black, red, or white cloth. This space is laid out in a semicircle, which is completed as a full circle by the playing area. The stage props also indicate that a ritual will take place: a calabash of palm wine on a stool, a large mortar and pestle, a bamboo bed with the body of Ntep Iliga (the late reigning chief), and three stools for the performers, also covered with a black, red, or white cloth.

When Ngond Libii, the chief's wife, enters the space, she sings a funeral song, and is later joined by a chorus of women. She moves to the calabash and goes through the motions of blessing the body of her husband. As his surviving wife, she must both honor his body and spirit and face the responsibility of causing his death. Their eldest son, Ntep Ntep, accompanies the mourning song with drumbeats. As this rhythm intensifies, the chorus of women "close their eyes, dancing in ecstasy" (59). The ritual of resurrection ensues, and the dead chief rises to bless the community in the play and performance space with "peace," "love," "energy" and "power," and to release his wife from punishment for his death (59–60).

Through the play, Liking draws on the goddess's power to bring peace to a community in a time of mourning in order to reimagine the position of the widow. Ngond Libii has literally been defined by her husband, the chief: her name means "the woman enslaved by Ntep Iliga." Ntep Iliga was revered in the community; yet, as Ngond Libii reveals, her husband spent his time drinking palm wine and lazing around, rather than working to earn money for their household. According to tradition, she must sacrifice herself for him. However, if he did not succeed in his duties as her husband in life, then why, she asks, should he be honored in death? Instead, she alters the funerary proceedings and empowers herself in the process.

She establishes herself by accompanying the chanting of the Hilun the griot with her own direct address to her husband and to the crowd gathered. Griots (griottes for women) are traditional storytellers and historians who know thousands of verses and local histories; they are trained musicians or singers, entertainers capable of improvising for their crowd, and even peacekeepers in West African societies. The role of the griot may be inherited or, increasingly, learned as a trade. Some griots play musical instruments including the stringed kora, drums such as the djembe or dundun, or the balafon (a keyboard-like instrument with resonating gourds); some are singers. Most notably this play, Ngond Libii accompanies her son's drumming, assuming the rhythm as she pounds a pestle into a mortar powerfully and incessantly. Traditionally, only men could beat drums in West African societies. Drumming communicates with the spirits, and because women were considered dirty during menstruation, they were not allowed to drum. Therefore, Ngond Libii's action flies in the face of conventional gender roles. She converts a woman's instrument of domestic labor—the mortar and pestle—and the chore of pounding grains for food preparation into an act of protest. Simply including the mortar and pestle in the sacred space defies the divisions between the private and public spheres, between the perceived place of the woman in the home and the male-exclusive community center. Ngond Libii claims her voice publicly. In this way, the widow forces all around her to reconsider their practices which privilege the existence of men—even when dead—over the living women.

By reinventing ritual aspects that engage both audience and performers, Liking's play and its performance offers another sense of "universal knowledge," both preserving Pan-African traditions and prompting audiences to reassess society and restrictive gender roles.

Fig. 5.2 L'arbre dieu. Werewere Liking and Ki-Yi Dance, 2017. Photo courtesy Werewere Liking.

Sogolon

While *The Power of Um* focuses on a wife–husband relationship, *Sogolon* looks at a mother–son relationship. The 2006 play's full title is *Sogolon, l'épopée panafricaine, ou la vie ordinaire d'une femme épique* [Sogolon, Pan-African Epic, or the Ordinary Life of an Epic Woman]. In it, Liking rewrites the epic of Soundiata, founder of the Malian Empire. This was one of the largest empires in West Africa that flourished from 1226 to 1670 and became well known for its trade, particularly in gold. Soundiata was banished from the kingdom he was to inherit and spent years in the forest, growing strength and knowledge from the animals and his mother, until he finally returned to claim his rightful place and build an empire. In Liking's version of the play, she not only innovates the story's form but also its content to tell the story of Soundiata's mother, Sogolon. Thus, as a woman playwright, Liking revises one of the most important African myths about a man and told traditionally by male griots by placing a woman at the center.

In her telling, Liking emphasizes the royal mother's part in her son's successes. He would not have succeeded without her magical healing powers that cured his inability to walk and guided him through his exile, his fight for the throne, and his further conquests. The story of Soundiata is well known and serves as a model for younger generations. Here, however, the lessons are revised, because "by making women central, Liking gives them a voice and calls attention to their concerns as wives, mothers, and citizens" (Denyer 89). She also honors them by connecting the mythical figure of Sogolon, a sorceress, to the traditional priestesses of Bassa and to contemporary women and their powers to cultivate life.

In the physical storytelling for *Sogolon*, Liking also takes on the male-exclusive puppetry tradition of Sogo bò. "Sogo bò" means "the animals come forth" in Bamana, the language most widely spoken in the present-day country of Mali. The full-body puppets used in Sogo bò are crafted from wood and cloth, generally representing animals important to the Bamana and Bozo peoples of Mali. (Among the Bozo, the tradition is called *do bò*, meaning "the secrets are presented.") The former are traditionally hunters who used the puppetry to celebrate successful hunts with puppets such as chimpanzees, birds, and snakes. The Bozo people are fishermen, so their puppetry might be performed from canoes and feature fish and crocodile puppets. The name Sogo bò also evokes the most important animal of the puppetry tradition: the antelope. The antelope is a highly revered animal for the Bamana, for, according to legend, a part-antelope, part-human being called Ci Wara taught the people the secrets to agricultural cultivation. The Malian legendary figures of Soundiata and Sogolon also connect to animal symbolism, as he was known as "the Lion King" and she "the Buffalo Woman."

Traditionally, young men between 13 and 15 years old are initiated into the Sogo bò practice as members of a *kamelon ton* association, where they learn the secrets of carving and performing in the full-body puppets. Like many practices, this tradition has specific roles for men and women. Men carve the puppets from the wood of sacred trees and perform as the puppets. Women accompany performances through song and may play small percussive instruments.[1] Each performer's identity remains hidden, as their bodies are completely covered during performance. In 1977, Liking traveled to Mali to be the first woman to study with legendary puppetry artist Yaya Coulibaly, who has created and collected hundreds of puppets and shared them internationally through exhibitions with his troupe, coincidentally called Sogolon. It was Coulibaly who helped Handspring Puppetry Company of South Africa develop their full-body puppets for *The Tall Horse* in 2004.

In Liking's *Sogolon*, the title character is a human puppet with buffalo horns. She performs alongside full-body puppets of humans, horses, antelopes, and a lion, in addition to cow and buffalo puppets performed by children, some wearing stilts. Thus, the stage space is filled with larger-than-life characters reflective of both the Malian tradition and the epic stature of Sogolon and Soundiata. Similar to the puppet forms in Sogo bò, the puppet bodies are largely draped cloth over frames of wood; Liking added screens in the cloth to facilitate the performers' ability to see when performing on indoor stage spaces—an innovation from the traditional puppet performances that happen outside during daylight and are guided in their movements by musicians. While the necks and heads of the puppets are traditionally carved from wood, Liking chose a combination of wood and papier-mâché, a much lighter material. Nevertheless, the resemblance to the Malian model is evident in the puppets created by Liking and Ki-Yi Mbock. This honoring of a cultural tradition from another part of Africa illustrates Liking's interest in creating Pan-African theatre. Through *Sogolon*, she aims to not only retell a foundational myth by centering a woman erased from history, but also reinvigorate traditional West African storytelling forms for younger generations.

As in *The Power of Um*, storytelling techniques in *Sogolon* lend themselves to ritual qualities. For example, the back of the stage area is decked with transparent veils to represent the curtain of the past through which the backstory scenes play out. Twelve songs narrate the story accompanied by the visual element of the puppets. Further, Liking starts with a

Hijingo ritual dance in which audience members and performers are invited to be active participants and to spin round and round to achieve a trance-like state of clarity. In this way, all present—performers and audience members—are equal community members, prepared to share this performance and knowledge of the universe. By reappropriating traditions and rituals in this manner, Liking emphasizes the role of women priestesses as in the Bassa rituals she learned as a child. She moves women's power from the private sphere to the public: the stage. This, in turn, empowers all women present to partake in the storytelling and myth-shaping that subverts patriarchal expectations and centers women.

WRITING AS A MISOVIRE

These works demonstrate how Werewere Liking incorporates African traditions and contemporary gender issues to develop ritual theatre experiences that raise up women. Many women writing from Africa eschew the term "feminist" because of its connections to white French and US women's movements and politics. For this reason, in discussing African women's movements, the term "Womanism" is often applied. Unlike feminism, which promotes gender equality, African womanisms embrace a notion of complementarity between gender roles in society. For example, in many West African societies, men conventionally dominate agricultural work while women often play a more prominent role in the marketplace. Still, wives and mothers might determine what is planted; men may also sell food and other products. What is key to understanding gender roles in West Africa is that they are not defined in terms of a gender binary. Liking also developed her own term—*misovire*—to promote her view of society. Taking on the western term misogynist, or "women hater," she writes not as a "man hater" as the literal translation of *misovire* would be; rather she writes as someone who denounces patriarchal social practices that diminish women. By rewriting and foregrounding the role of women and by redefining rituals and revising traditions in her work, Liking has created new possibilities for a complementary existence and representation of women with men.

French scholar Valerie Orlando explains that "in the late 1970s women were still left without voice and unaccounted for in the wings of dramatic productions in West Africa. It is from this wasteland of feminine artistic deprivation that Werewere Liking has emerged" (156). Whereas several women novelists writing in French emerged in West Africa around this time, Liking was alone in theatre. Her work paved the way for other women theatre-makers to speak out and create for the stage in Central and West Africa. Burkinabè playwright Sophie Heidi Kam completed a workshop with Liking early in her career and has now published multiple volumes of poetry and plays. In 2019, Lionelle Edoxi Gnoula's one-woman show, *L.E.G.S.* won the Prix Maeterlinck in Brussels. In 2022, the work of Senegalese playwright Penda Diouf, *Pistes*, toured in France, Germany, and the US. Nathalie Hounvo-Yekpè of Benin and Afi Marie-Josée Gbegbi of Togo both premiered plays in Avignon, France, at the famed theatre festival. From Liking's legacy, women writers are redefining theatre in their own terms, in their own voices, alongside women performers onstage.

TESS ONWUEME

One of Africa's leading female playwrights, Tess Onwueme hails from the Eastern Nigerian town of Ogwashi-Uku in Delta State. Born on August 8, 1955, she attended the Mary Mount College, Agbor, and graduated from the University of Ife in 1979 with a degree in Education English, and in 1982 with a Master's degree in literature. She obtained her PhD in Literature from the University of Benin in 1987. Though she was the second published female playwright in Nigeria after Zulu Sofola, she is the most popular female playwright in the country and indeed one of the most popular playwrights in Africa.

Onwueme has won many awards and recognitions both nationally and internationally. Four of her plays have won the Association of Nigerian Authors (ANA) Literary Prize for Drama: *The Desert Encroaches* in 1985, *Tell it to Women: An Epic Drama for Women* in 1995, *Shakara: Dance Hall Queen* in 2001, and *Then She Said It* in 2003. In 2000,

Fig. 5.3 Tess Onwueme. Photograph courtesy of Tess Onwueme.

she won a Ford Foundation Research Grant for her writing project titled "Who Can Silence Her Drum: Delta Women Speak," and in 2001, she received a second Ford Foundation Grant for the stage production of her drama, *Then She Said It*. It is important to note that all four award-winning plays, with the exception of *The Desert Encroaches*, address the condition of women in society, especially their quest for identity and power.

Onwueme's plays have been performed not only in Africa, but also in the United Kingdom, Canada, the USA, India, and the Caribbean. Her play, *The Broken Calabash* had a successful premiere at the Bonstelle Theatre at Wayne State University in Detroit, Michigan. In 2001, *The Missing Face* was staged off-Broadway at Woodie King, Jr.'s New Federal Theatre, and *The Reign of Wazobia* was adapted to film in 2000.

The Broken Calabash and *The Reign of Wazobia* are the first and second plays in what is known as the Trilogy of the She-Kings, the last being *Parables for a Season*. These three plays feature heroines who are educated and use their voices to challenge extant cultural practices that undermine women's achievement in modern society.

The Broken Calabash (1984)

The Broken Calabash examines inheritance, legacy, power, and gender; however, the play particularly challenges the culture of *Idegbe* that denies a girl the freedom to choose her husband. The story centers on Ona, a university undergraduate and only child of Chief Eloke Rapu and his wife Oliaku of the Ogwashi-Uku community. Traditionally, male children propagate the family lineage, while young women would normally marry and support their husbands' families. However, when a family has no male heir, culture dictates that one of the daughters becomes an Idegbe—an unmarried girl who remains in her father's house to produce children (ideally males) to extend her family lineage.[2] Or, instead of having children, she could marry another woman to fulfill that obligation. Being an only child and a girl, this duty rests squarely on Ona's shoulders. She has to produce an heir to inherit the family land and property. However, as a contemporary university student who knows her rights and cherishes her freedom, Ona opposes this tradition. Thus, Ona rejects the idea of serving as an Idegbe and insists on marrying Diaku, the man she is in love with. She is also not considering the second option to marry another woman to fulfill that task. Further complicating Ona's decision is Diaku's status as an osu (an outcast). It is taboo for a freeborn like Ona to marry an osu in Ogwashi-Uku, and in fact the whole of

Igboland. When Diaku arrives with his people to start the marriage process, the negotiation ends badly, and the calabash of wine brought by the intended in-laws is broken, which portends a bad omen in Igbo culture.

Consequently, Diaku marries Ugo, Ona's best friend and Ona resolves to deal with her father: "Yes, yes, my father has at last succeeded in ruining my life. But I will show him. Ona will show him pepper ... yes, yes, I am going to implicate him ... Yes ...Yes ... the wheel must come right round" (112). Thereafter, she claims to be pregnant by her father. This false accusation of incest coming from his own child leaves her father no choice but to take his life. All this takes place during the Ine festival when the land is purged of evil people, which then prompts the question: Is Courtuma evil to Ogwashi-Uku?

The Reign of Wazobia (1988)

At the start of this play, the monarch of Anioma's kingdom is dead. It is the custom of the land to choose a female regent who will reign for three years before the next king is crowned. This choice falls on Wazobia, a young university graduate from a poor parentage. For both Wazobia and Ona, their level of education empowers them with the intellectual acumen to argue their stand against moribund cultural norms. However, the surrounding attitude toward women in politics is starkly revealed by Chief Idehen's statement: "Serious matters of state concern are too heavy for the brittle heads of women and children" (27).

Contrary to tradition, Wazobia begins to make changes in the kingdom. Particularly, she reviews many of the customs that are oppressive to women. Most significantly, she gives as much recognition to women as she gives to men. As the king regent, Wazobia inherits not just the palace but also the palace wives—the late king's wives. Against the normalized hierarchical and patriarchal practices of the land, Wazobia sits at the same level with her wives and talks with them as equals. Also, it is the custom that when a king dies his wives

Fig. 5.4 Opening Glee for *Reign of Wazobia,* October 14, 2014, Schofield Hall, University of Wisconsin. Photo courtesy of the playwright.

will dance naked around the market to prove that they had no hand in his death. However, when the Omu, the leader of women, reminds Wazobia that it is time for the palace wives to perform this widowhood ceremony, Wazobia declares that henceforth women will not perform the inhuman widowhood practices from which men are exempted (*Reign of Wazobia* 18). In her democratization initiative, Wazobia also upturns another social norm by inviting not only women, but also youths to village meetings. She even goes as far as to change the symbol of the community to a palm tree, to symbolize a true democracy where everybody is recognized and appreciated. She explains that no part of a palm tree is useless; therefore under the democratic dispensation, a palm tree is a very appropriate symbol for the community henceforth (*Reign of Wazobia* 32).

Wazobia's decisions and radical consideration of gendered norms in the traditions and structures of leadership meet with some resistance. Iyase, who by tradition should be the next king, demonstrates his rejection by refusing to bow to her until he is forced to. Idehen, who is third in command, also rejects Wazobia's leadership, because of her poor parentage and the fact that she is a king surrogate, whom he sees as overstepping her bounds. Though Omu is the leader of the women, she is opposed to the changes Wazobia is making to improve the conditions of women. Omu views her duty as that of a custodian of culture and protector of the status quo.

Consequently, Wazobia faces resistance from men and women in the community, and these conservatives led by Iyase, demand her removal from the throne. Her duty as a king regent is to hold the office until the next king is crowned; she does not have the constitutional right to change anything. In response, Wazobia argues that it is sexist to place a woman on the throne but rob her of the political power that goes with it, and she refuses to accept half-measures. Since the gods have chosen her to be there, she is determined to rule totally and actively. In her fight against sexual discrimination in her kingdom, Wazobia wants to exercise full power and full tenure as a king.

After all attempts to eliminate Wazobia fail, the conspirators force the Chief Priest to present the traditional pot of rejection to her. This means that Wazobia must not only abdicate the throne but also die by suicide. She defiantly refuses. Instead, through persuasive speeches and intellectual reasoning, she tries to win Omu over to her side with no apparent success. It is not until the men arrive with the pot of rejection that Omu's change of heart is made evident to both Wazobia and the audience. It is a different Omu that we see in the end—one who leads the women to battle against the men in support of Wazobia's continued stay on the throne. The protesting women, all naked, storm the stage, and the men, overwhelmed by the nakedness of the women, retreat. Culturally, women use their nakedness as a last resort to gain attention to their protest. It never fails because of its cultural implications.[3]

The Reign of Wazobia is one of the most powerful feminist dramas written by Onwueme, presenting and redefining women in power and politics. It has had several editions in 1993, 2000, and 2014, and an electronic version of the play was produced in 2016, under the title *Wazobia Reigns*.

Critical Responses to Onwueme's Gendered Ideology

Tess Onwueme is one of the most studied Nigerian female playwrights, and many scholars have explored the ways that she addresses contemporary and traditional gendered social and political roles in Nigeria. Writing about Onwueme's Trilogy of the She-Kings, Eugene Redmond declares that "in Onwueme's soular system, women cannot be reduced to a group of quarrelling chicks" (17).

Mabel Evwierhoma's study of ten of Onwueme's plays focuses specifically on the power and powerlessness of women both in Nigerian society and Onwueme's creative works. According to Evwierhoma, Onwueme's plays contain "the most inspired manifestations, to date, of the feminist and womanist perspective in contemporary Nigerian drama created by female writers" (viii). Nolas-Alausa also reflects on Onwueme's accommodationist approach to feminist agitation which she achieves "without the attendant uproar that constitutes such agitations in other climes;" this, for him, is an indication that "African feminist ideology differs from its Western counterparts" (2).

In her political plays, such as *The Reign of Wazobia* and others, we see the oppressed people—invariably youths and women—rise in opposition to their oppressors. This is a common theme in Onwueme's work, as she encourages the oppressed to fight for their rights. She believes that if a situation must improve, it must be by the efforts of the victims.

All the forces that Onwueme responds to in her plays are agents of sociopolitical imbalances that lead invariably to the marginalization and oppression of minority groups in society. Thus, Onwueme fights for social justice on diverse fronts. She has fought against injustice against women in *The Broken Calabash, The Reign of Wazobia, Parables for a Season,* and other plays. She has also fought racial discrimination against Black people in *The Missing Face*, exploitation of young academics in *Mirror for Campus*, and exploitation and dehumanization of minority groups in less developed countries of the world in *The Desert Encroaches*.

A daring woman, Tess Onwueme lends her voice to the liberation of women and other marginalized groups. She will be known as the first radical female playwright in Nigeria because she is the first to critically reappraise the conditions of women in society and the first to take bold steps to reposition women in the political realms where they previously were sidelined.

CONCLUSION

Tess Onwueme and Werewere Liking are two contemporary pioneers in West African feminist, womanist playwriting. They ventured into the hitherto male-dominated field of theatre and used their theatrical works to make women seen and heard in mainstream African cultural spaces—spaces where women have traditionally been silenced and excluded. Onwueme is the second published female playwright in Nigeria, but the first to challenge the image of women in theatre and the culturally assigned role of women in society. Her plays consistently interrogate and subvert negative images of women, and she boldly renegotiates and redefines topics such as modernity, education, human rights, and globalization. Likewise, Werewere Liking, through her plays, reinvents traditional rituals by creating space for women in them and offering female-centered re-readings of traditional stories. In addition to being an internationally lauded playwright, she created Ki-Yi Mbock to train and promote the younger generations of West African artists. In the theatres of both women, age-old cultural practices that impede women's progress are confronted and dismantled to pave the way for women's development and empowerment. The strong new images of women created by these West African female dramatists have gradually replaced the stereotypical images of the powerless, voiceless, and marginalized women historically prevalent in African dramatic writing. These new possibilities for independent and liberated African womanhood make Liking and Onwueme significant voices in African, and specifically West African theatre, and their works are key touchstones to be read, studied, and performed around the world.

FURTHER RESOURCES

Aragbuwa, A. "A Comparative Study of Female Transgressors in Tess Onwueme's *The Broken Calabash* and the *Reign of Wazobia*: A Feminist Critical Discourse Analytical Perspective." *International Journal on Studies in English Language and Literature (IJSELL)*, vol. 6, no. 8, 2018, pp. 50–61.
This paper compares Wazobia and Ona as female transgressors and underscores the importance of women's solidarity in the fight for women's emancipation.

Udengwu, Ngozi. *Contemporary Nigerian Female Playwrights: A Study in Ideology and Themes*. LAP LAMBERT Academic Publishing, 2012.
This documents the plays of seven Nigerian female playwrights who, like Onwueme, promote the image of women in dramatic literature.

Denyer, Heather. "Werewere Liking, Vicky Tsikplonou, and Adama Lucie Bacco: Female Artists Appropriating Puppetry to Empower Women in West Africa." *Woman and Puppetry: Critical and Historical Investigations*, ed. Alissa Mello, Claudia Orenstein, and Cariad Astles. Routledge, 2019, pp. 85–100.
This chapter in a volume dedicated to women puppetry artists discusses three West African artists and how they have subverted the male dominant traditions in creating puppetry that empowers women and girls today.

Morgan, J.C., and I.A. D'Almeida, eds. *The Original Explosion that Created Worlds: Essays on Werewere Liking's Art and Writings*. Brill, 2010.
This comprehensive collection of essays looks at the entirety of Liking's work up to 2010. It is the only the one of its kind and establishes her place in West African art and literature.

Liking, W. "African Odyssey: Village Ki-Yi M'bock". Kennedy Center feature, 1997. https://www.kennedy-center.org/video/education/music-world/african-odyssey-village-ki-yi-mbock. Accessed December 17, 2023.
Liking and members of the Ki-Yi Mbock troupe visited a high school in Virginia. Watch their plays told through traditional African song and dance.

Onwueme, Tess. "Erupting Silences: Dr. Tess Onwueme Speaks/ Performs the Soul of Africana," filmed at Villanova University, Pennsylvania, 2012. https://www.youtube.com/watch?v=jmKFX5 pi7XA. Accessed July 22, 2023. Dr. Onwueme addressed the Africana Studies Department at Villanova University and shared about her work.

REFERENCES

Denyer, Heather. "Werewere Liking: Claiming Puppetry Traditions for Africa's Future." *Puppetry International*, vol. 37, 2015, pp. 10–13.

Dunton, C. *Make Man Talk True: Nigerian Drama in English Since 1970*. Hans Zell Publishers, 1992.

Evwierhoma, M. *Female Empowerment & Dramatic Creativity in Nigeria*. Caltop Publications, 2002.

Liking, Werewere. *The Power of Um; and, A New Earth: African Ritual Theatre*. Trans. Jeanne Dingome et al. International Scholars Publications, 1996.

Liking, Werewere. Personal interview, 2017.

Marzette, DeLinda. *Africana Women Writers: Performing Diaspora, Staging Healing*. Studies on Themes and Motifs in Literature Series. Peter Lang US, 2013.

Mielly, Michelle. "An Interview with Werewere Liking at the Ki-Yi Village, Abidjan, Côte d'Ivoire, 2 June, 2002." *African Post-colonial Literature in English*. https://www.postcolonialweb. org/africa/cameroon/liking/2.html. Accessed April 20, 2023.

Nolas-Alausa, T. "The African Woman and Feminism: A Study of Two Selected Texts by Tess Onwueme." Babcock University Gender Association. *Journal of Gender Studies*, 2012, pp. 1–18.

Onwueme, Tess. *The Reign of Wazobia*. Heinemann Educational Books, 1988.

———. *The Broken Calabash*. Heinemann Educational Books, 1984.

Orlando, Valerie. "Werewere Liking and the Development of Ritual Theatre in Cameroon: Towards a New Feminine Theatre for Africa." *African Theatre for Development: Art for Self-Determination*, ed. Kamal Salhi. Intellect, 1988, pp. 155–174.

Redmond, E. "Tess Onwueme's Soular System: Trilogy of the She-kings—Parables, Reigns, Calabashes." *Tess Onwueme's Three Plays*. Wayne State University Press, 1993, pp. 12–18.

Worugji, G. "Redefinition of the Position of Women in Osonye Tess Onwueme's Play *The Reign of Wazobia*." *Lwati: A Journal of Contemporary Research*, vol. 7, no. 2, 2010, pp. 196–205.

NOTES

1 A good example of a performance tradition with defined male and female roles is Yoruban masked dance, Gẹlẹdẹ.
2 Call it prostitution of sorts, but that is not the way it is regarded. The father of the children has no rights over them, even if he knows about them. They have the same surname as the Idegbe.
3 For more, see Naminata Diabate's book, *Naked Agency: Genital Cursing and Biopolitics in Africa* (2020).

CHAPTER 6

Crossing Borders and Transforming Gender Identities

Mahesh Dattani and Manjula Padmanabhan

Jashodhara Sen

In recent decades, young Indian women have increased visibility in popular media forums by participating in international beauty pageantry. Among them, Harnaaz Sandhu discussed her plans as Miss Universe 2021. Sandhu said:

> My advocacy is regarding women empowerment, and for this, [...] I have been focusing on my community because I have seen how my mother has dealt with a patriarchal system. I would like to talk about empowerment all around the world, [...] we need to take action now, then only can we look forward to the future. (Chimah)

Sandhu, a 21-year-old woman, represents contemporary India and vocalizes the ongoing need for gender equity on a global platform. Her invitation to foster a resilient community is an intersectional call emphasizing a cross-border, intergenerational dialogue about gender in India.

Identified as a secular, sovereign, and democratic nation, India has a rich and complex history of colonization, migration, and succession. With its political system as a democratic republic following its independence from Britain in 1947, India inhabits a paradox that encompasses concepts like secularism, gender equity, social justice, and national development. The paradox

DOI: 10.4324/9781003272854-7

is rooted in India's internal unequal systems, such as the caste system, a classification system for dividing labor and power among people in Indian society. While the struggle to eliminate caste-based discrimination within the Indian community continues, other forms of inequality, such as class and gender, are deeply steeped in the caste system. The plays discussed in this chapter, *Dance Like a Man* (1989) by Mahesh Dattani and *Harvest* (1997) by Manjula Padmanabhan, confront the binary matrix of heteronormative power that exists with the caste system and a changing Indian society, both illuminating the sociological interaction between gender and theatre.

Both Dattani and Padmanabhan's plays portray the characteristics of modern Indian theatre, which emerged tentatively in the late 1970s.[1] It is important to note that the contemporary Indian theatre repertory is characterized by its multidimensionality, which includes a variety of styles, genres, and content. While many theatre history courses in the US and other Western nations include classical Sanskrit drama or Kathakali dance-drama, there is often less attention paid to the development of modern Indian plays and the ways in which they draw from various historical cultural performance traditions as well as deviate, in part due to the impact of colonialism. Another aspect to consider in modern Indian theatre is the import of language and accessibility—some plays are in Bengali, others in English, still others in Hindi, Marathi, Gujarati, and Tamil. Additionally, according to Farley Richmond, modern Indian theatre is primarily urban rather than rural and "created by and primarily for people who may be regarded as middle and upper middle class" (387). Keeping in mind Richmond's contention, both *Dance Like a Man* and *Harvest* are written by urban playwrights and depict the lives and tribulations of modern urban Indian families.

This chapter investigates how two prominent modern Indian playwrights, Dattani and Padmanabhan, use their work to interrogate social implications of gender that rely on a heterosexual binary within both an Indian and global context. The plays differ in their content, with Padmanabhan's *Harvest* emphasizing the connection between gender and commodification in *Harvest* and *Dance Like a Man* examining the politics of power in patriarchic, traditional, yet transitional postcolonial Indian society.

Besides gender and sexuality, in the context of South Asia, and more specifically India, caste becomes an unavoidable discussion. Contextualizing **gender stratification** (or the inequalities that exist among genders—typically men and women, although further and necessarily complicated by nonbinary and gender nonconforming identities—in regard to wealth, power, and privilege), and patriarchal structure within the caste–class dynamic is critical for studying gender and understanding these plays within this cultural context. The caste system in India, historically known as *varna* but more accurately represented as *jati*, is a social hierarchy that has been a significant part of Indian society of centuries. It categorizes people into different groups or castes based on their occupation, social status, and birth, and is rooted in endogamy, or marrying within the limits of a particular community or group. It is important to note that the caste system is a complex and deeply ingrained aspect of Indian society, and any discussions about it often involve historical, cultural, and political dimensions.

Within this chapter, I employ a **Third World feminist**[2] lens to look at the plays' "traditional" and cultural contexts, calling attention to the patriarchal construction of "preservation" of "tradition" and the "selective and problematic ways in which these 'traditions' are understood" (Narayan 29). While there are multiple definitions and types of "feminism," it is important to note that feminism did *not* originate in white European society. Third World and transnational feminisms encourage us to think beyond white "second-wave" feminist views that are commonly associated with the 1960s and have historically considered oppression tied to whiteness and gender in the West. Feminist scholars such as Chanda Talpade Mohanty and Uma Narayan use "Third World" to reclaim and reappropriate the term, which allows previously colonized people to recognize their political opposition and resistance. Transnational and Third World feminists also prompt us to be aware of the distinctions between "First World" and "Third World" women, urging us to critically consider the diversity of feminist movements across the world. According to Narayan, anyone who challenges the heteronormative matrix of gender and sexuality also challenges tradition and actively destabilizes patriarchal **hegemony**, which is often viewed as a threat to cultural gatekeepers.

Rigidly preserving traditional ideas to retain gender-specific occupations and roles is an intergenerational crisis in India. This concept is tied to upholding Indian cultural identity associated with traditional family values. According to Nita Kumar, "South Asia has its own discourse of gender and power," historically and deeply informed by colonialism (12). In postcolonial India, gender role stereotyping and gender differences are two sides of the same coin, and they are perpetuated by popular media such as newspaper ads, television, and films. Shoma Munshi observes that advertising of the 1990s constructed the image of the "New Woman," indulging a sense of modernity yet tradition in terms of caregiving and bearing household responsibilities for urban Indian women (575). This fixed sociocultural identity determines femininity and reinforces a binary construction of gender, which in turn influences how "men" should or shouldn't act in private and public spaces. These systems are commonly non-negotiable in personal and familial settings where power relations are unequal based on people's gender identity, and it is also the first introduction to how to be a certain gender is taught.

GENDER BEYOND THE BINARY IN *DANCE LIKE A MAN*

Centering on unequal power relations, gendered bodies, and cultural conflict, Mahesh Dattani's play *Dance Like a Man* subverts the fixed construction of gender roles and critiques the patriarchal and antiquated social structures. Mahesh Dattani, a contemporary Indian playwright, director, scholar, and recipient of numerous literary accolades, is one of the most prominent Indian playwrights writing in English and is known for his socially conscious plays. His plays, such as *Tara* (1990), *On a Muggy Night in Mumbai* (1998), and *The Big Fat City* (2012), are frequently set in the modern urban Indian landscape and critique patriarchy through the juxtaposition of gendered relationships. Most of his plays, including *Dance Like a Man*, are set in postcolonial India, exposing the country's cultural contradictions under the guise of tradition and modernity.

First performed in Bangalore in 1989, *Dance Like a Man* parallels the intricate relationships between three generations: professional dancers Jairaj and Ratna; their daughter Lata and her fiancé Viswas; and Jairaj's father, Amritlal. Moving from the 1940s to 1990s, the play alternates between the past and the present, delving into generational family dynamics and the sacrifices that Jairaj and Ratna make to pursue their dreams of becoming professional Bharatnatyam dancers. Amritlal does not support their dance training, and he especially opposes Jairaj's plans because he feels dance makes his son less of a man. We also see these gendered expectations echo through generations in Lata, Jairaj and Ratna's daughter, who has grown up in the shadow of her parents' unfulfilled dreams and herself is an aspiring dancer. In *Dance Like a Man*, Dattani highlights how beliefs about the gendered nature of dance and its relationship to sexuality are still evident in contemporary Indian society. While Jairaj and Ratna were direct victims of Amritlal's authoritative voice, the forced gender norms within the familial and larger heteropatriarchal structure continue to dictate Lata's career in dance in modern urban India of the 1990s, raising questions about societal expectations, gender roles, and the price of individual aspirations in a traditional and conservative society.

In the play, several traditional types of Indian dance are featured. Jairaj and Ratna are Bharatnatyam[3] dancers, and Jairaj wants to continue his training in Kuchipudi dance. Kuchipudi dance in particular becomes an epitome of dismantling gender normativity. A historically complex dance form originated in Andhra Pradesh (South India), the Kuchipudi dance is immersed in Hindu spirituality, making it a significant cultural institution that carries great, longstanding meaning. According to dance scholar Rumya S. Putcha, contemporary Kuchipudi shares aesthetic characteristics and a vocabulary of movements similar to other South Indian dance forms like Bharatnatyam (92). Putcha points out that, in the

Fig. 6.1 Debjani Banerjee and Anil Joseph in *Dance Like a Man,* directed by Mahesh Dattani (ICS Theatre, East Brunswick, NJ). Photo by Kousik Bhowal.

mid-twentieth century, there was a lack of female representation in Kuchipudi, with the exception of actress Kanchanamala and a few devadasi[4] performers whose surnames were not included in programs. As a result, the male dancers popularized the practice of female impersonation, or strī vesaṃ (103). In *Dance Like a Man,* Jairaj Parekh pursues Kuchipudi dance against his father's wishes. His father associates dance with femininity and an inherent threat to masculinity. By placing the play within the historically gendered world of Kuchipudi dance, Dattani not only engages with binary ideas of men and women's roles but also questions strict considerations of heterosexuality.

The portrayal of gender discrimination in *Dance Like a Man* also reflects the social and political climate of post-independence India and the ways that gender and sexuality are linked to political movements and progressive ideas. Several radical movements emerged in India during the 1960s and 1970s, from student protests and labor agitations to peasant uprisings and anti-caste, tribal, and consumer movements.

These movements included a range of political ideologies, from Gandhian socialism (a form of socialism based on the theories of Mahatma Gandhi featuring overtly moral principles of equal living and working conditions and advocating nonviolent protest) to far-left agitations (Kumar 20). The far-left political movements in particular spurred discussions about gender equity, specifically stressing how religious teachings oppress women and people from lower castes and socio-economically deprived classes. However, these activist groups lacked cohesion and their ideas became muddled among the urban, educated middle class (21). Ironically, both in India and *Dance Like a Man*, reformist ideas failed to both change people's minds and challenge the prevailing social construct for everybody, not just the so-called urban elite or educated class.

For instance, Amritlal, despite his progressive ideas of social reform and Indian independence in the 1940s, rejects his son Jairaj's wish to join his wife Ratna as a Bharatnatyam and Kuchipudi dancer. In a heated argument, Amritlal asks Jairaj, "Why must you dance? It doesn't give you any income. Is it because of your wife? Is she forcing you to dance?" (Dattani 37). Amritlal's questions reveal a generation's fixation on dance as an unsuitable profession for men because it is financially unviable as well as the assumption it is too feminine. In response, Jairaj declares, "Nobody's forcing me," articulating his agency and free will to be a dancer (37). Amritlal is unaffected by his son's declaration, and the conversation illustrates the futility of the culturally constructed and fragmented notion of "progressivism" in middle-class, post-independence India. Jairaj ultimately observes to his father, "Where is the spirit of revolution? You didn't fight to gain independence. You fought for power in your hands. Why, you are just as conservative and prudish as the people who were ruling over us!" (37).

Amritlal's traditional perspective also extends to Jairaj's wife, Ratna. While his prejudicial behavior restrains Jairaj's freedom to dance as a man, he alludes to something more unwarranted regarding his daughter-in-law Ratna: Amritlal compares dance with prostitution. He accuses Ratna of visiting a devadasi named Chenni amma every Monday. According to Avanthi Meduri, devadasi women were "practitioners [...] who sang and danced in the courts and temples of South India in the nineteenth century" (12). They once held a high social status because dancing was essential to temple worship. Later, in colonial India in the 19th century, the devadasi and their dance, Sadir, were wrongly referred to as "temple prostitutes." By questioning Ratna's intention of visiting 75-year-old Chenni amma, one associated "with the old school," Amritlal links dance with prostitution (Dattani 42). Amritlal's comparison of dance to prostitution dehumanizes and alienates the female body from their artistic expression and calls into question women's agency in creating a life for themselves—an embodiment of heteropatriarchy. It also reveals that dance is considered feminine, and if reversed, feminine is then read as anti-masculine. In both cases, it does not fit the heteropatriarchal binary of traditional masculinity.

Through the play, Dattani examines how gender roles and binaristic ideas of gender impact women and men. On one hand, Jairaj liberated himself by going beyond the gender binary, disregarding the materiality of livelihood, and making dance the center of his life; on the other hand, he reduced himself to less of a man. During a conversation with Ratna, Amritlal asks, "Do you know where a man's happiness lies? [...] In being a man" (49). Jairaj's existence as a human is called into question by his presence as a dancer, which directly conflicts with the patriarchal, heteronormative male identity, according to Amritlal's definition of manhood. Dattani emphasizes that men, too, can be oppressed and suppressed by the strict, binaristic gender roles and expectations of society.

One last illustration of the complexity of gender roles in *Dance Like a Man* is in Jairaj and Ratna's daughter Lata, a young, successful dancer navigating the politics of the dance world. While Ratna uses her contacts and resources to help Lata advance her career, she also lives vicariously through Lata. Lata's success is Ratna's way of challenging patriarchal bounds: "[S]he is on her way to fame which is what I wanted for her. She had my blessings and guidance and now that her performance has been noticed by the right people, it shouldn't be very difficult for her" (64). Unlike Ratna, Lata can *decide* to continue a career in dance. In contrast, Ratna obtains her right to her daughter's success by default of motherhood. As her daughter's nurturer and caretaker, Ratna fulfills heteropatriarchal requirements only by serving as the means of reproduction—a wife and mother.

As one of Dattani's most produced and taught plays, *Dance Like a Man* offers a consideration of the performance of gender and its evolution within paradoxes regulated by the systems of power. Jairaj's life is shaped by patriarchal oppression, much like Ratna and Lata. He challenged and, to some extent, subverted the binary of masculinity and femininity. However, while he resisted heteropatriarchy via his dancing, when he becomes a father, the role is reversed (Pramanik 234). Fatherhood comes with the social expectation that Jairaj will be a provider and protector. If he fails to perform these duties, he risks being invalidated and excluded from the patriarchy. Consequently, Jairaj is fully aware of the complexities involved in his daughter choosing dance as a career and a non-dancer as her life partner. He understands the consequences of not following socially constructed rules. As such, it seems Jairaj willingly submits to patriarchy for Lata's success as a dancer within heteropatriarchal norms. Through *Dance Like a Man* and his other plays such as *Tara,* about conjoined male and female twins, and *Bravely Fought the Queen*, about gender, family, and featuring a gay character, Mahesh Dattani depicts the conflicting reality of modern, urban Indian society and families and ultimately, much like Jairaj, hopes to push audiences to move beyond a binary and destabilize the social, traditional, and limiting construction of genders.

PERFORMING SUBJECTHOOD IN *HARVEST*

While Mahesh Dattani's yearning for a just world in *Dance Like a Man* considers the past and present, Manjula Padmanabhan and her play *Harvest* looks to a futuristic, dystopian Third World, which unites patriarchal power and the exploitation of gendered bodies under the pretext of modernity and scientific advancement as perpetrated by First World on the Third World.

In 1997, as India celebrated 50 years of independence, Manjula Padmanabhan's *Harvest* won first prize in the first Onassis Cultural Competition for Theatre and premiered in Athens, Greece, at the Teatro Texnis. It has since been included in several international play anthologies, and in 2001, director Govind Nihalani adapted the play into a film called *Deham* (or *The Body*). Artistically, Padmanabhan wears many hats, working as a playwright, illustrator, and journalist. As the daughter of a diplomat, Padmanabhan grew up in many countries, which shaped her cross-cultural understanding of nations and identity. Padmanabhan addresses various themes in her writings, including social exclusion and marginalization, violence against women, and urbanization in postcolonial India. In a conversation with *The Indian Express*'s Amrita Dutta, Padmanabhan stated:

> I was brought up with very few restrictions. I had no awareness that there might be restrictions on my freedom, I didn't even think of it as liberating. I had no idea that women occupied a sort of specialised domain, or that what lay ahead of you—for 99 percent of the world's women—are marriage and motherhood.

When asked whether she is deliberately "challenging gender-based/biased sociocultural boundaries" in her work, Padmanabhan responded:

> Maybe. I think it's possible that I position myself a little differently compared to my contemporaries. I grew up away from my home-culture and by the time I returned to India, my consciousness had set in a mold that was not (and is not) wholly Indian. I don't think of myself as Indian or even as a woman—even though I know, OF COURSE, that the world sees me within those two definitions. (Pandey 4)

Padmanabhan's response alludes to her insider/outsider point of view, symbolizing the multiplicity of selfhood. By assuming this nuanced position, Padmanabhan challenges patriarchal-endorsed stereotypes of gender, sexuality, and nationality—a critical lens evident in *Harvest*. A transnational tale, *Harvest*, seeks to reveal "some of the corporeal and cognitive dimensions of globalisation and to ask questions about the ways in which it affects race and ethnicity as they are currently conceived, and performed" (Gilbert 123). Simultaneously, *Harvest* focuses on local issues, such as how, fueled by poverty, Third World subjects, particularly women, become victims of international trafficking via human body organs. *Harvest* portrays power disparities on multiple levels, showcasing the giver–receiver dynamic and the commodification of gender.

Just as Mahesh Dattani draws on urban settings in many of his plays, *Harvest* is set in 2010 Bombay (present-day Mumbai), a city that is home to numerous multinational corporations as well as one of the world's largest slums: Dharavi, located on Bombay's outskirts. The power disparity in this geographical location is consistent with the power relations in *Harvest*, in which the contemporary **capitalist economy** determines the fate of the impoverished and heightens other aspects of inequality. Manjula Padmanabhan's timely intervention highlights hegemonic power relations through scientific innovations and the commodification of human bodies. People are reduced to nothing more than organs by the insatiable appetite for capitalist profit-making.

The story is about a family of four: Om Prakash, a young unemployed man who lives with his wife Jaya, his mother Ma, and his younger brother, 17-year-old Jeetu. Jeetu supports the family through sex work. The play opens with Ma and Jaya's conversation in which the mother holds power over Jaya, her daughter-in-law. The familial power dynamic slowly unfolds to reveal adversarial relationships between the family members. Although unemployed, Om is the dominant patriarchal representation in his family, a position supported by Ma. In contrast, Jeetu's position is vulnerable; his brother and mother despise him. Due to her status as a dependent Third World woman, Jaya is at the bottom of this domestic hierarchy. In her character description Jaya is labeled and stereotyped as a disadvantaged, oppressed woman from a Third World country

(Padmanabhan 5). However, this is a simplistic, generalized view of the character. As Chandra Talpade Mohanty argues, Third World women "do not represent any automatic unitary group," just as "Western women" or "white women" cannot be characterized as a homogenous group (7). The aforementioned "groups" necessarily contain alliances and divisions based on factors such as class, religion, sexuality, and history. Jaya exists, for example, among the opposing forces of racism, sexism, colonialism, and imperialism. Jaya's situation is compounded at home, with a dictatorial mother-in-law and an indifferent husband who signs off on her body for the global market, rendering her disposable at the whim of male ownership and daily by her closest relatives. Padmanabhan deftly situates Jaya within a paradigm in which Jaya's fate is dictated by racially superior, imperially minded, sexually controlled actions. The character Jaya and *Harvest* is a reminder that women's subjecthood and experience with patriarchal oppression are not linear or homogenous. By placing "organ transplantation and reproductive science (and, by implication, the transnational adoption trade in third-world babies) on a continuum that suggests the ways in which interested capital penetrates the very corpus of its multiple and diverse subjects," Padmanabhan addresses many interlocking issues, from the explosion of tech-based communication to the First World's cannibalistic ambition to consume the Third World which frequently centers and destroys gendered bodies (Gilbert 125). While the way in which Ratna in *Dance Like a Man* deals with cultural violence differs from the way Jaya confronts the danger of Om's arrangement with InterPlanta in *Harvest*, both playwrights and plays consider the transnational, transcultural, and intergenerational ways that gender informs people's experiences in modern India—an experience also echoed by Harnaaz Sandhu's more contemporary call for continued global consideration and transnational action to combat systems of oppression.

In *Harvest*, Om signs a Faustian contract with a multinational biotechnology company, InterPlanta Services, to serve as an organ donor for North American people. Om will receive substantial compensation for this "job," and to ensure his eligibility as a donor, his family's standard of living will be raised to First World standards. Which part of his body is donated to InterPlanta is unspecified; hence, Om's entire body and, by extension, his very existence are at the disposal of the company. InterPlanta installs surveillance systems to closely observe Om's domestic sphere, and:

> the installation of these new products requires a complete removal of all third-world implements from Om's flat. Modern technology, therefore, is not a passive additive element to the Third World; it is an invasive controlling force that renders obsolete and destroys all existing modes of knowledge use in the third world. (Mathur 128)

The Prakash family's anxiety sets in as they do not know the true purpose of these gadgets or "Contact Modules" to establish a connection between the donor and the receiver. The intense chain of events that follows jeopardizes the entire family's fate.

It is perhaps useful to note that although the play is specifically set in Bombay with an Indian donor and North American receivers, Padmanabhan advises that others "should take on the racial identities, names, costumes, and accents most suited to the location of the production," with this, she prompts artists and audiences to consider both the specific Indian perspective and larger global scope and impact of the issue (Padmanabhan 6).

First, a blonde American girl, Ginni (or Genie), the prospective recipient of the body parts, enters Prakash's home. Ginni is a virtual manifestation, "a computer-animated wet dream" who speaks in a "sweet and sexy" voice (Padmanabhan 84, 6). The sexualization of Ginni, along with her identity as not only American but also as a blonde (and presumably white) woman offers both commentary on the supposed allure of American capitalism but also the power of whiteness. What's more, Ginni's invasion—even in this virtual manifestation— is nothing less than **settler colonization**, entering a space and dictating how these Indians should live their daily lives. Through the character of Ginni, Padmanabhan reveals the colonial desire to dominate Third World bodies.

When InterPlanta agents arrive to take him for transplant, Om escapes and endangers his family. Instead of taking Om, they capture his brother Jeetu, as Om had planned. The transplantation is successful for Jeetu's recipient but leaves Jeetu partially blinded, and when the InterPlanta agents come again for more, it results in Jeetu's death. Here, we realize Jeetu is viewed as disposable to his brother and mother. This sense of disposability is tied to Jeetu's work as a sex worker, which is often considered a feminized profession. As a result, Jeetu's disposability (and feminization) is comparable that depicted in *Dance Like a Man* and the ways in which "tradition" is often tied to strict, binaristic ideas of gender as enforced by patriarchy. Both *Harvest* and *Dance Like a Man* expose the commodification and negotiation of gender to destabilize historically constructed gendered categories and to question development in Indian and global contexts.

While Dattani's work considers tradition and gender vis-à-vis classical Indian dance and middle-class families, in *Harvest,* Padmanabhan employs contemporary, technological lenses. In addition to Ginni's need for Jeetu, as the story unfolds, Jaya's Third World body becomes desired by Virgil, a white American man. The harvesting of and desire for Third World women's bodies serves the first-world patriarchy under the guise of modern machines. Ziauddin Sardar notes that cyberspace is emerging as the new Other of Western civilization, projecting all its colonial prejudices, as well as the images of sex and violence with which it has framed non-Western cultures, onto cyberspace, and thus "the occupation of cyberspace has direct parallels with the colonisation of non-Western cultures" (777). Sardar argues that the capitalist, materialist nature of cyberspace ensures that the marginalized remain marginalized, always exploited by those with more resources and money (788). As Virgil attempts to seduce her, Jaya must utilize increasingly more desperate measures, including threatening to take her own life. Ultimately the marginalized stays marginalized in *Harvest*, as illustrated by Mathur, "the donors are thus conquered through a reinforcement of sexual divisions through the patriarchal gaze of modern science" (130).

Fig. 6.2 *Harvest* produced by Ethnic Cultural Theatre in Seattle, WA, directed by Lydia Fort, sets by Czerton Lim, lights by Jeremy Winchester, costumes by Katie Goodman. Photo by Czerton Lim.

Jaya's existence is a testament to women's historical feminist, antiracist, and nationalist struggles, particularly in India. In the final scene, Jaya dialogues with Virgil, and the West/East, First World/Third World gendered dichotomy is once again visible, with cannibalistic imperialist ideals devouring their colonized subjects and their reality. M.K. Rukhaya points out that Virgil means "flourishing" in Latin and is an amalgamation of the terms "virgin" and "vigil" (82). In this play, Virgil represents the flourishing of **neo-imperialism** and its insidious, deep impact on gendered relationships (82). When Virgil appears, his voice is described as an "American cigarette commercial accent—rich and smoky, attractive and rugged," but the body is Jeetu's (Padmanabhan 6). The disparity between American and Indian (South Asian) cyber-representation draws on an array of inequalities, including economic, biological, technological, and social inequalities, in which an American's existence, although artificial, precedes and takes over a Third World individual.

Jaya, however, is not taken in by the virtual "non"-reality. When the time comes to begin the surrogacy, Jaya threatens to take her own life if she is forced to do anything without her consent and declares, "If I lose my life, I win this game" (91). Jaya's refusal to cede decision-making power to Virgil, a symbol of the imperial heteropatriarchy, allows her to take control of her own fate, destabilizing both patriarchy and Western imperialism. Her demands are necessary for establishing a relationship between the First World and the Third World based on basic human dignity, and it begins with convincing Virgil to say her name correctly. Jaya's position as an unfulfilled, exhausted wife whose only job is to serve her family is subverted at this point, and Jaya emerges as an empowered Third World woman who is not afraid to challenge the patriarchy or imperialist, capitalist structures of oppression.

CONCLUSION

Dattani and Padmanabhan are two key voices in modern Indian theatre whose works, *Dance Like a Man* and *Harvest*, serve as touchstones with their groundbreaking depictions of contemporary urban life in India that envision a future for Indian families liberated from social discrimination and stigma. Simultaneously, these notable playwrights steered the development of English language theatre in India by subtly shifting Eurocentric canons toward Indian and transnational perspectives, particularly emphasizing the impacts on gendered bodies. They join and have created space for other notable English-language playwrights such as Poile Sengupta, Kusum Kumar, Anupama Chandrashekhar, and Akarsh Khurana.

There are many parallels in Dattani and Padmanabhan's work as evidenced in *Dance Like a Man* and *Harvest*, such as intergenerational conflict and enduring as well as overcoming gender-based violence, and both playwrights use their work to demand a permanent change in the way patriarchy and imperialism operate in urban spaces. While independence offers the opportunity for progress and development, once-colonized nations also live caught between the power imposed by colonization and its legacy. As a result, preserving traditional values becomes synonymous with preserving one's independent identity in a postcolonial country, which directly opposes colonial progressivism.

In Jairaj's resistance of the traditional and patriarchal perspective of fixed gender roles in classical dance, he engendered space for young women, allowing his daughter Lata to continue her dance career; in Jaya's decision to retain her independence, she speaks to the resistance of the Third World against other, imperialist cultures. Similarly, today, Harnaaz Sandhu (former Miss Universe) keeps her promise and continues her work towards gender equity in India, influencing policy-making and challenging the stigma surrounding women's menstrual health. Sandhu, like Jairaj and Jaya as well as Dattani and Padmanabhan, challenged strictly gendered roles and actively cultivated a more equitable, inclusive space for the next generation.

FURTHER RESOURCES

Dalmia, Vashudha. *Poetics, Plays, and Performances: The Politics of Modern Indian Theatre.* Oxford University Press, 2008.
A useful examination of the political and aesthetic development of modern Indian theatre, starting from 1870s through the 1970s.
Dharwadker, Aparna. "Modern Indian Theatre." *Routledge Handbook of Asian Theatre.* Routledge, 2016, pp. 243–267.
A concise but rich overview of qualities of modern Indian theatre.
Singh, Anita. "Aesthetics of Indian Feminist Theatre." *Rupkatha Journal on Interdisciplinary Studies of Humanities,* vol. 1, 2009, pp. 150–170.
A foundational look at feminist Indian plays, written by men and women, during the 1900s to early 2000s. It offers useful context on the feminist movement in India and a sense of the many languages feminist Indian dramatists use.
Mohanty, Chandra Talpade. "Under Western Eyes: Feminist Scholarship and Colonial Discourses." *Boundary,* vols. 12/13, 1984, pp. 333–358. https://doi.org/10.2307/302821.
Mohanty's article is a foundational text in establishing and articulating Third World and transnational feminist ideas.

Spivak, Gayatri Chakravorty. "Diasporas Old and New: Women in the Transnational World." *Textual Practice*, vol. 10, no. 2, 1996, pp. 245–269.
A postcolonial theorist, Spivak is another early and key voice in Third World and transnational feminist discourse.

REFERENCES

Chimah, Hesha. "Harnaaz Sandhu Speaks about Her Miss India to Miss Universe Journey. Exclusive!" *Times of India*, December 22, 2021. https://timesofindia.indiatimes.com/life-style/fashion/buzz/harnaaz-sandhu-speaks-about-her-miss-india-to-miss-universe-journey-exclusive/articleshow/88438921.cms. Accessed December 30, 2023.

Dattani, Mahesh. *Dance Like a Man: A Stage Play in Two Acts.* Penguin Books India, 2006.

Dutta, Amrita. "And Still I Rise: Why Manjula Padmanabhan Never Came to Terms Being the Second Sex." *The Indian Express*, October 4, 2015. https://indianexpress.com/article/lifestyle/books/and-still-i-rise-why-manjula-padmanabhan-never-came-to-terms-being-the-second-sex. Accessed December 30, 2023.

Gilbert, Helen. "Manjula Padmanabhan's *Harvest*: Global Techno-scapes and the International Trade in Human Body Organs." *Contemporary Theatre Review*, vol. 16, no. 1, 2006, pp. 123–130.

Kumar, Radha. "Contemporary Indian Feminism." *Feminist Review*, vol. 33, no. 1, 1989, pp. 20–29.

Mathur, Suchitra. "Caught between the Goddess and the Cyborg: Third-World Women and the politics of Science in Three Works of Indian Science Fiction." *Journal of Commonwealth Literature*, vol. 39, no. 3, 2004, pp. 119–138.

Meduri, Avanthi. "Bharatanatyam as a Global Dance: Some Issues in Research, Teaching, and Practice." *Dance Research Journal*, vol. 36, no. 2, 2004, pp. 11–29.

Mohanty, Talpade Chandra et al. *Third World Women and the Politics of Feminism*. Indiana University Press, 1991.

Munshi, Shoma. "Wife/mother/daughter-in-law: Multiple Avatars of Homemaker in 1990s Indian Advertising." *Media, Culture & Society*, vol. 20, no. 4, 1998, pp. 573–591.

Narayan, Uma. *Dislocating Cultures: Identities, Traditions, and Third World Feminism*. Taylor & Francis, 2013.

Padmanabhan, Manjula. *Harvest*. Aurora Metro Books, 2003.

Pandey, Rachana. "In Conversation with Manjula Padmanabhan." *Muse India*, March–April 2018. https://museindia.com/Home/ViewContentData?arttype=feature&issid=78&menuid=7707. Accessed December 30, 2023.

Pramanik, Amlan Roy. "Dance Like a Man beyond the Discourse of Gender: Relocating the Tragedy of Jairaj in the Circumscribed World of Politics and Power." *International Journal of English Literature and Social Sciences*, vol. 6, no. 1, 2021, pp. 231–234.

Putcha, Rumya S. "Between History and Historiography: The Origins of Classical Kuchipudi Dance." *Dance Research Journal*, vol. 45, no. 3, 2013, pp. 91–110.

Richmond, Farley P. "Characteristics of the Modern Theatre." *Indian Theatre: Traditions of Performance*, ed. Farley P. Richmond, Darius Swann, and Phillip Zarilli. Motilal Banarsidass Publishers, 1993, pp. 387–461.

Rukhaya, M. "Dispossessing Reality: Manjula Padmanabhan's *Harvest*." *International Journal on Multicultural Literature*, vol. 5, no. 2 (2015). pp. 77–84.

Sangari, Kumkum. "The Politics of the Possible." *Cultural Critique*, vol. 7 (1987), pp. 157–186.

Sardar, Ziauddin. "alt.civilizations.faq Cyberspace as the Darker Side of the West." *Futures*, vol. 27, no. 7, 1995, pp. 777–794. https://doi.org/10.1016/0016-3287(95)80008-W.

NOTES

1 For a better understanding of modernity, contemporaneity, and postcoloniality in relation to drama and the historicization of "Indian theatre," see Aparna Dharwadker's work *Theatres of Independence: Drama, Theory, and Urban Performance in India since 1947*, University of Iowa Press, 2009.

2 According to Kumkum Sangari, "Third World" is a term that emerged in the 1950s and "both signifies and blurs the functioning of an economic, political, and imaginary geography able to unite vast and vastly differentiated areas of the world into a single 'underdeveloped' terrain" (158).

3 Bharatnatyam dance originated in the southern Indian states of Tamilnadu and Chennai and is one of the most well-known classical dance styles still practiced in India.

4 Literally "servants of God", devadasis are women who performed dances as part of rituals associated with temples.

CHAPTER 7

Staging Indigenous Women's Voices, Histories, and Power

Yvette Nolan and Emily A. Rollie

As theatre artists, we are storytellers. Particularly in **Indigenous** creation and performance, stories and storytelling are "a method of knowledge production and connection" and stories link us to the world, to each other, to our histories, and to the future (Syron 57). As Cree scholar Margaret Kovach writes, "oral stories are born of connections within the world and are thus recounted relationally. They tie us to our past and provide a basis for continuity with future generations" (94).

Indigenous laws and teachings are also embedded in our stories. I (Yvette) did a session with Maria Campbell for the Canadian Institute for the Administration of Justice in 2015 in which we animated one of our Elder Brother stories to show how they directly connect to Indigenous justice and teachings—this to a room of 250 lawyers, judges, and law students.

This essay, too, began in dialogue. Before setting words to paper, we—Yvette Nolan and Emily Rollie—engaged in conversation, discussing the legacy and key points in the constellation of Indigenous drama and Indigenous women's drama in Canada. We acknowledge our individual positionalities and different experiences—Yvette as Algonquin Canadian artist-scholar, and Emily as an American scholar of Canadian theatre and feminist director. Within that, we also recognize our overlaps and points of connection, of shared interest. Much like this text seeks connections between key points or touchstones in a larger constellation of staging genders as a way to place ourselves as readers and artists within our ever-evolving theatrical legacies, the conversation between

DOI: 10.4324/9781003272854-8

the two of us provided a point of overlap and connection, a moment of knowledge sharing and intercultural, transnational storytelling of Indigenous women's performance history.

INDIGENOUS PLAYWRITING AND GENDER

Early inclusion of **First Nations** drama and plays in modern and contemporary Canadian theatre tends to focus on male theatre-makers such as Tomson Highway, Kevin Loring, and others. Highway's *Dry Lips Oughta Move to Kapuskasing* (1989), for instance, is included in *Modern Canadian Plays*, a prominent anthology of Canadian drama, making it a key example and often one of the only representative Indigenous plays. Similarly, Highway's *The Rez Sisters* (1986) is commonly referenced, appearing often in course syllabi and anthologies.

While these are undoubtedly key voices and powerful leaders in the emergence of written, Indigenous drama in English, Indigenous women writing plays and performing hold a particular (and powerful) place in Canadian and North American dramatic history and performance studies. After all, "Just being in the world as an Indigenous woman is a political act. Refusing to be silenced or disappeared is political" (*ROOM Magazine*). This chapter is then an effort to acknowledge the longstanding and contemporary efforts of Indigenous women theatre-makers—playwrights, directors, performers, dancers, and others—to create theatre as an act of resistance, an act of sharing stories and making sure those stories are not forgotten but find life and kinship through performance.

Of course, it is important to articulate that part of this consideration of the "canon" of Indigenous drama is also often reliant on a white, settler colonial conception of "performance" and "plays" that privileges the written word and printed texts (and in English). It often overlooks other forms of storytelling and performance based in orality and other embodied (and often Indigenous) formats. Instead, perhaps it is more useful to echo the phrase used in a 2014 Summit of 12 Indigenous theatre leaders who gathered in Banff to discuss the previous 30 years of Indigenous theatre/performance; they crafted a list (available as an appendix in *Medicine Shows*) and called it, simply, "body of work" (Nolan 5).

We also recognize that in this discussion of gender in Indigenous drama acknowledgement must be paid to queer and **two spirit** artists, who have long been creators in the Indigenous theatrical world but have perhaps been silenced even more within the white settler-colonial heteronormative patriarchal structures that inform theatre-making practices across **Turtle Island**. As the editors of *Critical Companion to Native American and First Nations Theatre and Performance* (2020) note, "Indeed, there would be no American or Canadian theatre were it not for Native peoples, cultures, stories, and the lands from which they arose" (Darby et al 4). As such, we recognize and honor the diversity of Indigenous experiences, lives, and cultural traditions—a challenge to chapters like this in which we must synthesize and summarize. With over a thousand federally-recognized Indigenous nations and tribes across Turtle Island, in a single essay we cannot speak to every Indigenous identity, each of which has its own language (or languages), culture, rituals and spiritual practices, and relationships to the settler–colonial structures and policies that surround it. We can, however, point to and reflect on values that are common across many nations: relationship to land, the community over the individual, and (ironically) the recognition of the role of women.

ANNIE MAE'S MOVEMENT

First performed in 1998 via an independent production in Whitehorse, Yukon, *Annie Mae's Movement* then was performed at On the Waterfront Festival in Halifax, Nova Scotia, before its publication by Playwrights Canada Press in 2006. Produced In 2001 by Native Earth Performing Arts, Canada's longest-running professional Indigenous theatre company, the play was remounted in 2008 for a tour in Aotearoa (or New Zealand in te reo Maori) and Australia.

Then and in the years since, *Annie Mae's Movement* has been regularly pointed to as a key moment in Canadian as well as in First Nations theatre. It is included in multiple anthologies, including volume 2 of *Staging Coyote's Dream: An Anthology of First Nations Staging Drama in English* (Mojica and Knowles), and the play is one of the key case studies in Sarah MacKenzie's *Indigenous Women's Theatre in Canada: A Mechanism of Decolonization*. Regularly taught in classrooms, the play is often identified as an integral, important piece of Canadian theatre history and highlighted in interviews such as Canada's Theatre Museum video series (available on YouTube).

The play joins the work of other Indigenous playwrights such as Marie Clements (whose play *The Unnatural and Accidental Woman* also explores violence against women in Vancouver, British Columbia), Monique Mojica (who wrote *Chocolate Woman Dreams the Milky Way* and many others) and the more contemporary Tara Beagan, Falen Johnson, Yolanda Bonnell, and Frances Koncan.

Annie Mae's Movement focuses on the life and work of Mi'kmaq (Micmac) First Nations woman Anna Mae Aquash, an Indigenous activist who became a key figure in the American Indian Movement (AIM) that began in Minneapolis, Minnesota, in 1968. The real-life Anna Mae moved to the United States from Nova Scotia in the early 1970s to work with AIM, and rose quickly through the ranks of the male-dominated organization, becoming a target of the FBI because of her activism and strong voice. She disappeared in winter 1975, and in February 1976, a rancher found a woman's body on South Dakota's Pine Ridge Reservation, a body later identified as Anna Mae Aquash. A second autopsy revealed that Aquash had been murdered, but her case went uninvestigated, effectively silencing her story, for many years. It wasn't until 2004 that a conviction was made for Aquash's murder.

The play *Annie Mae's Movement* came out of a conversation I (Yvette) had at an opening night of a play in Winnipeg.

Standing around with a couple of Indigenous women, we said to each other, "When are we going to see a play that *we* want to see?" We started talking about Annie Mae Aquash, and Joanna Brandt's book *The Life and Death of Anna Mae Aquash* (1993) which had just come out. We were excited about the thought of telling her story before she disappeared from the public eye and historical record. Of course, at that point in time, in 1996, her murder was not solved; it was not even being investigated. As an artist and woman, I wanted to give her voice. I wanted people to not forget her.

The play asks larger questions about history and the value of life, the value of stories, the value of the individual, and the value of community. It speaks to the specific historical event as well as the larger, often-ignored and ongoing global phenomenon of Missing and Murdered Indigenous Women and Girls (MMIWG). In fact, Annie Mae's opening words in the play point to just that:

> There are all kinds of ways of getting rid of people. In Central America they disappeared people. Just came and took them away in the middle of the night, whoosh gone, and then deny everything. Very effective. Well, here they disappear too. They disappear them by keeping them underfed, keeping them poor, prone to sickness and disease. They disappear them into jails. In jails they disappear their dignity, their pride. They disappear our kids, scoop 'em up, adopt 'em out. (Nolan 2)

From the start, Anna Mae demands the audience consider absences, disappearances, and silences on multiple levels. She refers to the disappearance of people during Argentina's "Dirty War" which occurred during the 1970s and early 1980s (and is referenced in regard to Griselda Gambaro's work in Chapter 4 of this volume); she points to high numbers of Indigenous people incarcerated or simply underfed amid inequitable governmental and social policies and forced relocation to under-resourced reservations; she references what became known as the "Sixties Scoop"—the mass and forced removal of Indigenous children from their families and placed

Fig. 7.1 Sophie Merasty in the original production of *Annie Mae's Movement*. Hardly Art, Whitehorse, Yukon, Canada, 1998. Photo by Philip Adams.

into residential schools and into Euro-Canadian families. Annie Mae continues:

> It's so easy to disappear people in this country, especially Indian people. Scoop 'em up here, drop 'em off there. Whoosh, gone. Then just deny everything.
>
> Anna Mae? Anna Mae Who? Never heard of her...
>
> Whoosh...
>
> *She is gone.* (2)

To all of these silences, Annie Mae's story adds yet another—the disappearance of Anna Mae herself and of other Indigenous women.

The play, however, was challenged by people because there is a singular woman in the center of it; then there's the man who plays all the other roles, all of the other men. Many people said, "You're being cheap. It's about economy and not hiring too many actors." But I (Yvette) responded, "No, actually, all of those men can be each other." Within the Western, white patriarchal structures, all of those men can be each other, and any man can be that powerful and destructive. As such, Anna Mae is the focus, the woman at the center of it all. That artistic choice problematizes her relationship to her community and the movement. She's fighting for her people, which are Indigenous folk, but she goes to the **American Indian Movement** in the United States and works with a pan-Indian group. Even within that group of her people, she then is disenfranchised by the men because the patriarchy exists.

Someone once said to me (Yvette) that Indigenous women are at the bottom of the pecking order: There's white men, then white women, then Indigenous men, and then Indigenous women. That's the order of things and that we have seen manifested in the **Murdered and Missing Indigenous Women and Girls (MMIWG)** movement in North America. When I went to Aotearoa to work with my Maori colleagues, they asked: "You have an acronym? MMIWG? You actually have a shorthand term for what happens to Indigenous women?" I didn't realize how strange that was.

Annie Mae appeared before we had the term Missing and Murdered Indigenous Women and Girls, but she was—she *is*— part of all of those murdered and missing Indigenous women's stories. She's working for her people who are all Indigenous people. But she is working mostly for her daughters, even though it means leaving them. The fact that, at the end of the play, you can't tell which man is threatening her, or whether it is all the men who are responsible for her and her murder. I wrote the play in 1996, but nothing has changed in that much time. I look at the play today, and it is still sadly relevant.

Indeed, the play depicts the multiple intersections that both the real-life figure of Anna Mae and the character in the play inhabit as a First Nations woman in a white man's world, a Canadian in the United States, and a woman in a male-dominant movement of the American Indian Movement. Once I started writing

Annie Mae, she brought all these other women into the room with her, and I brought them all into the play, too. For instance, she talks about her mother in the opening monologue:

[W]e should learn to fight. And because we'd never get enough firearms, we had to use the only thing that they couldn't take away from us. We had to train our bodies, [...] I guess I got it from my mother, she used to fight with the Indian Agent. [...] You gotta stand up, you gotta fight for what's important, no matter who wants to shut you up. (Nolan 2)

Then, in the final monologue, she names all those women:

My name is Anna Mae Pictou Aquash, Micmac/ Mi'kmaq Nation from Shubenacadie, Nova Scotia. My mother is Mary Ellen Pictou, my father is Francis Thomas Levi, my sisters are Rebecca Julien and Mary Lafford, my brother is Francis. My daughters are Denise and Deborah. You cannot kill us all. You can kill me, but my sisters live, my daughters live. You cannot kill us all. My sisters live. Becky and Mary, Helen and Priscilla, Janet and Raven, Sylvia, Ellen, Pelajia, Agnes, Monica, Edie, Jessica, Gloria and Lisa and Muriel, Monique, Joy and Tina, Margo, Maria, Beatrice, Minnie, April, Colleen... (68)

In the end, Annie Mae names her family—her mother, daughters, and sisters, and as a playwright, I named all of the women who, at that point in my life, had influenced me artistically, my artistic ancestors. Some of my family are named in that list alongside Annie Mae's family. We are building and naming our community and our ancestors. Even in that final moment of death, she brings in all the women and vows, "You can kill me, but you cannot kill us all" (68).

CIRCULARITY AND COMMUNITY AS INDIGENOUS, FEMINIST STRUCTURES AND PRACTICES

In *Annie Mae's Movement,* I (Yvette) was trying to tell stories in a different way as well as tell different stories, and so that idea of circularity. We start with Annie Mae and we end with

Annie Mae—it is a moment in her life. We have talked about that structure with different designers: about what happens between the opening monologue and the closing monologue? Is it between the time the trigger is pulled and the bullet arrives? Is it flashback? Is it memory? We have to use all of the rules of other theaters, such as Western canonical theater, to try to figure out what we are doing and at the same time not be constrained by it.

In dramatizing Aquash's story, *Annie Mae's Movement* grounds itself initially in realism but then quickly expands to become more, becoming mythical—employing the Indigenous figure of the Rugaru, a half man half wolf creature. Often affiliated with the **Métis** and Cree traditions and sometimes linked to the Windigo (Anishinabe) or Jinu (Mi'kmaq), the Rugaru (or rougarou) was said to roam the woods, perhaps as a caution to children not to venture too far from home. Described in the play as "part man, part creature, big and hairy, obviously not of this world. [...] There is something of the animal about him. Canine. Lupine. Something of the supernatural, the ability to be here, and then suddenly there," the Rugaru haunts the periphery of Annie Mae's story and the audience's consciousness (3). The presence of a creature "not of this world" reminds the audience of connections to the spirit world, and challenges their perceptions of this world, and of Annie Mae's story.

In terms of working in Indigenous practice, it is always about being part of a community more than an individual. As a director and artist, I (Yvette) am always making a triangle. Then I tip it on its side and I squash it, and it becomes a circle.[1] That's how we work. It seems so simple and so self-evident, but it can be challenging because it requires more conversation. It requires more relationality. It requires more time. It is fascinating how people will push back against that structure, including us. Someone is always trying to push the circle back up on its side because then you don't have to take responsibility if there is someone at the top saying, "Do this, do that." When it is in this circular shape, everybody is responsible for holding the space and coming to the table. So in *Annie Mae's Movement*, we are focusing on a singular, unique woman.

But we're talking about the relationship to community, to the larger Indigenous community, whether that is the Toronto Indigenous community or the national Indigenous community or an international one.

Liza-Mare Syron echoes the importance of community and relationality in her study of the rehearsal practices used by Indigenous women artists in Australia, Aotearoa (New Zealand), and Turtle Island (North America): "what we know and how we approach research is often defined by our relationality. We belong to a community or communities where we have roles, status, and positions, which come with responsibilities and obligations to those communities" (2–3). There's always an awareness of responsibility and that we are creating art on behalf of our communities. There's responsibility, yet still we have to bravely do the work. For the women who have played Annie Mae, it is a clear journey: mother, warrior, and all the things that women are—even though we are often stereotyped into one trope: the Virgin, the Whore, or the Madonna. Annie Mae brings an awareness that this woman is all of these things; therefore, all of us are, too. We can be all of these things.

However, *Annie Mae's Movement* not only grappled with images and the embodied stories and voices of Indigenous women; it also, through its structure and casting, also speaks to masculinity, patriarchy, and race in regard to men's roles. One of the things that happened in the between the first Native Earth production and the second Native Earth production was that I (Yvette) returned to it with a dramaturg and put in a much tougher scene. I had shied away from that in the first writing, so the scene where she's drunk and splashing ketchup on herself to pretend that she's harming herself was not in the original production. This is the gift of returning to work after a period of time: It is being braver about it. That more challenging scene went in, and it complicates the story because everything should be that complicated for the man, the singular male actor who's playing all of the men. That's a hard job because they have to play white and they have to be Native. They have to be young and they have to be the law. They're being everything—such is the patriarchy and white supremacy—so they have to find those moments but continue to be in relationship. That part is always played by an Indigenous man. So the responsibility lies in that he has to learn to feel for the woman in the play, but also for the larger community of women.

Considering that embodiment of the patriarchy and the male voices surrounding her, it is no wonder the woman at the center of it is spinning out a bit. Because that's what we create, and the play moves that way. It is naturalistic at the start, and then it turns into a whirlwind so that at the end, when it is all those men surrounding Annie Mae, the audience does not know which specific men they are. They should be all of those men in one man. In fact, they also almost take on a larger, animalistic quality; in the stage directions during Annie Mae's final monologue, we see: "The man has entered and is watching her, smelling her. He is man, with elements of Lawrence, Dennis, FBI Guy, but he moves like an animal" (68). In this, audiences realize that this play is actually not only about Indigenous and non-Indigenous relations. It is actually about the patriarchy. It is about being a woman in a series of men's worlds. It is about patriarchy and power, and how we lose track of what the power does to us. It is also about the power of Annie Mae's voice, which had so much power that it needed to be silenced. Yet, she says, "You can't silence me." As an artist, I knew I was trying to keep her alive in a way that I didn't think she was going to. My intention was to keep her alive through art.

The play starts in realism and then evolves into something bigger, more metaphoric and symbolic, which makes the story also bigger than Anne Mae, but it still is her. Because we are never individuals, and we are always part of a community. She also was a teacher, so there's something about her being that role, a role traditionally considered a woman's role (at least at that stage of the game it was), and that being part of her identity. She is teaching both inside the play and outside the play. She is prompting people to look back at things like the Big Man, the Rugaru, the American Indian Movement.

All of those things that happen inside the play also extend outside of the play, just as life and art are intertwined.

One of the things that has happened in Indigenous communities is an articulation of the importance of the matriarchy, the importance of women. I (Yvette) have been to gatherings and round dances and demonstrations where male elders have stood up and said, "It is not our time, it is not our job. Men should be standing at the back and holding the women's backs." There's a sense of trying to rebalance things. There's a recognition that one of the "gifts" of colonization has been patriarchy. And we have ingested that as well. So men are trying to help to right that, and part of that work being recognition that women have a role and we have always had a role, but we have been pushed down. I think that has made a difference in terms of the way artists come to the work and the way women in particular come to the work. We talk about *Women of the Fur Trade*. It's called *WOMEN of the Fur Trade*. So there's an attempt to *write* and *right* history

Fig. 7.2 Monique Mojica, Michelle St John, Jani Lauzon, *The Scrubbing Project*, 2002, Turtle Gals Performance Ensemble. Photo by Nir Bareket.

to recognize the role of women in everything. We see it in so many pieces where women, particularly Indigenous women artists, are doing that work of rewriting history through performance such as Spiderwoman Theater, the longest-running Indigenous theatre company in the United States and founded in 1975 by Muriel Miguel, Lisa Mayo, Gloria Miguel, Lois Weaver, and Pam Verge, and Turtle Gals.

For me (Yvette), Turtle Gals are part of the genealogy, the constellation of Indigenous feminist theatre. Their work made such a big difference to my practice and to lots of artists' practice. It made us aware that there were other ways to create.

Composed of Jani Lauzon (Métis), Monique Mojica (Kuna and Rappahannock), and Michelle St. John (Wampanoag Nation), the Turtle Gals Performance Ensemble was best known for *The Scrubbing Project* (2002). Taken from the idea of scrubbing or cleaning oneself of their color, the performance explored the hilarious yet challenging experience of being a mixed Indigenous woman in the 21st century. *The Scrubbing Project* was directed by Muriel Miguel of Spiderwoman Theatre, who trained Turtle Gals in ensemble creation methods (Lauzon 90).

Of course, referencing Turtle Gals leads naturally to Native Earth Performing Arts, the longest-running Indigenous theatre company in Canada. Turtle Gals performed two pieces at Native Earth: *The Scrubbing Project (2002)* and *The Triple Truth* (2008), and I (Yvette) directed *The Only Good Indian* (2007) while serving as the Artistic Director for Native Earth from 2003 to 2011.[2] Founded in 1982, Native Earth Performing Arts is now a mainstay in Canadian theatre. Its first productions were collectively created, and one of which, *Double Take/ A Second Look*, was done in collaboration with New York's Spiderwoman Theatre and Tukak Theatret, a Danish company of Greenland Inuit theatre-makers.

If *Annie Mae's Movement* is a star in the constellation and lineage of Indigenous feminist theatre, what other artists' pieces are "milestones" or touchstones within that same constellation? With this, we are back to the idea of voices being erased, disappeared, or undervalued, but undoubtedly Marie Clements's work is the top. She is the best of us, and her *The Unnatural and Accidental Woman* (2005) pushes against the form and structures of performance. She writes big, epic pieces that have made the way for others to explore and innovate artistically. There was a period of time in Canadian theatre where there was only room for one Indigenous playwright, and it was always a man. It was Tomson Highway, then Kevin Loring, and it passed down because the mainstream decided that there could only be one. But women's work was very different from what the men were writing.

MILESTONES IN THE MAKING: *WOMEN OF THE FUR TRADE*

It's ironic. As we talk and write this essay in July 2023, we are both directing feminist, women-centered plays. I (Emily) am directing a feminist adaptation of Sherlock Holmes in Wisconsin, and I (Yvette) am at Stratford, the renowned Stratford Festival in Ontario, directing *Women of the Fur Trade*. Much like *Annie Mae's Movement*, it is also about women's stories that have been disappeared by history— disappeared by the men's stories. In this case, it is Louis Riel, Thomas Scott, and the history books. Although it has been over 20 years, we are still fighting to be heard.

Set in the late 1860s, amid the Red River Resistance—an uprising lead by the Métis (a term used to refer used to refer to a cultural group of people from mixed Indigenous and European heritage) against European colonizers, *Women of the Fur Trade*, written by Frances Koncan (Anishinaabe and Slovene from Couchiching First Nation), centers on three women's perspectives on the changing world around them— including colonization, the Métis leader Louis Riel, and, obviously, the fur trade.

The play and its production process brought both Indigenous working methods and stories to the longstanding Festival, known for its deep ties to Shakespeare and other

Fig. 7.3 Joelle Peters, Kathleen MacLean, Jenna-Lee Hyde in *Women of the Fur Trade* at Stratford Festival, Stratford, ON, 2023. Photo by David Hou.

"classic" works of the English and often European stage. While Indigenous artists and theatre technicians have worked at Stratford for many years, consistently holding and making space for other Indigenous artists to come through, *Women of the Fur Trade* was written about, created by, directed by, and (mostly) performed by Indigenous artists. Perhaps even more notably, *Women of the Fur Trade* also foregrounds, both in the title and play itself, the voices of Indigenous women.

These are generational stories. There is me, Yvette Nolan. Then there is Yolanda Bonnell, whose play *My Sister's Rage* was performed at Tarragon Stage (Toronto) in October 2022, and there's Frances Koncan and *Women of the Fur Trade*. We are all using performance to give voice to invisible stories, stories that, like MMIW, have been disappeared, and so many of those stories also address violence against gendered bodies. I am able to direct *Women of the Fur Trade* because those things haven't changed. Frances is coming at it from a millennial point of view that brings together contemporary speech with historical events and the women's intergenerational point of view, and Yolanda Bonnell's *My Sister's Rage* is so much about care—care of the women and the women in that community as well as about care of the community who comes to see the play. This way, we are working to not re-traumatize people, but to be able to expose these structures and issues so that we can do the work of healing.

We have always used humor. There's always been laughter. I think the shift may be also in an audience who is being given permission to receive things with humor. Which gives permission to the playwright and to the creators to make things funnier. *Women of the Fur Trade* is hilarious, yet we still get tears at the end. There is a turning point late in the play, and while there are still a few laughs, it helps people to open their heart with the laughter. We open them up, open them up with laughter, and then make our points while they are laughing.

These are women's works. They are part of a history of women and Indigenous women artists, and we have been creating for a long time while waiting for the world to catch up. Now the world is arriving and we are ready. And it is not only me who is ready. My descendants, my artistic descendants are also ready so when the moment arises there are more.

Perhaps the best way to describe Indigenous theatre and theatre-making is as circles upon circles. Or, as Darby et al. echo, ripples in a pond which reveal the ways that Indigenous plays "dip into ancestral wisdom and outward to the specific contemporaneous concerns of the audience" (10). This metaphor is echoed in *Medicine Shows: Indigenous Performance Culture* when thinking about writing in an Indigenous way *about* Indigenous performance: it is "dropping stones in a pond, watching the ripples move outward from the point of entry" (Nolan 4).

If a key component of Indigenous theatre is that Indigenous artists "maintain stewardship of their stories" (Syron 4), then works like *Annie Mae's Movement*, *Women of the Fur Trade*, *The Unnatural and Accidental Woman*, Turtle Gals, and others not only steward Indigenous stories, they also (perhaps more importantly) amplify, document, and illuminate

Indigenous *women's* stories—making sure their voices, these stories are not lost among the echoes of so many other stories on our stages and in our classrooms.

During the rehearsal process for *Women of the Fur Trade,* the visiting scholar Sara Pillatzki-Warzeha (Dakota) would bring in quotes from other scholars or share observations from her field notes as a way of reminding us why we were doing the work and what our responsibilities were to the story, to the ancestors, to each other. One of her offerings seems an apt final thought not only in regard to the constellation within which *Annie Mae's Movement* and these other Indigenous artists and pieces exist, but about the way we—Emily and Yvette— work together to share this knowledge: "It's not enough to claim relations with other peoples—we must consider what those relations ask of us, and how we may learn to be kin in ways that make one another's lives better" (Justice 82).

FURTHER RESOURCES

National Inquiry into Missing and Murdered Indigenous Women and Girls. *Reclaiming Power and Place: The Final Report of the National Inquiry into Missing and Murdered Indigenous Women and Girls.* June 2019. https://www.mmiwg-ffada.ca/final-report.
> The final report published by the Canadian National Inquiry into Missing and Murdered Indigenous Women and Girls. The Inquiry began in September 2016 and researched violence against Indigenous women, girls, and 2SLGBTQQIA (two spirit, lesbian, gay, bisexual, transgender, queer, questioning, intersex, asexual) people in Canada.

O'Hara, Jean Elizabeth, ed. *Two-Spirit Acts: Queer Indigenous Performances.* Playwrights Canada Press, 2013.
> An anthology of two-spirit art and plays written by two-spirit artists, specifically Waawaate Fobister, Muriel Miguel, and Kent Monkman.

"Indigenous Body of Work." Indigenous Performing Arts Alliance, https://ipaa.ca/resources/indigenous-body-of-work/. Accessed December 31, 2023.
> A dynamic, living document of performance works by First Nations, Métis, and Inuit artists across Turtle Island. The searchable list offers a combination of published play scripts and live productions of dance, music, and theatre—a way to push back against the primacy of published works (and English).

Mojica, Monique, and Ric Knowles, eds. *Staging Coyote's Dream: An Anthology of First Nations Drama in English*, vols. 1–2. Playwrights Canada Press, 2003 and 2009.

Curated and edited by Monique Mojica (Kuna and Rappahannock) and Ric Knowles, these anthologies were the first dedicated to Indigenous drama and performance in English. They feature plays by Indigenous theatre-makers across Turtle Island, such as *The Unnatural and Accidental Women* by Marie Clements and *The Independence of Eddie Rose* by William S. Yellow Robe, Jr. Vol. 1 features four plays by women Indigenous playwrights (out of nine plays total), and Vol. 2 includes *Annie Mae's Movement*, which is one of seven plays by women (out of ten) in the book.

Mojica, Monique, and Lindsay Lachance, eds. *Staging Coyote's Dream: An Anthology of First Nations Drama in English*, vol. 3. Playwrights Canada Press, 2023.

The third in the *Staging Coyote's Dream* anthology series, this volume features plays and offers culturally specific dramaturgical processes as models for relational artistic creation and land-based dramaturgies.

Nolan, Yvette, and Ric Knowles, *Performing Indigeneity*. Playwrights Canada Press, 2016.

An anthology of essays about Indigenous performance created to accompany the *Staging Coyote's Dream* plays. All contributors are Indigenous artists or academics.

REFERENCES

Canada's Theatre Museum. "Playwright Yvette Nolan." Interviewed by Andrew Moodie, 2015, https://www.youtube.com/playlist?list=PLgHeSy6OB4x72mEH_VoY5wkWeueKPXyFi. Accessed December 31, 2023.

Darby, Jaye T., Courtney Elikin Mohler, and Christy Stanlake. *Critical Companion to Native American and First Nations Theatre and Performance: Indigenous Spaces*. Methuen Drama, 2020.

Highway, Tomson. *Dry Lips Oughta Move to Kapuskasing*. In *Modern Canadian Plays*, vol. 2, 4th edn, ed. Jerry Wasserman. Talonbooks, 2000.

Justice, Daniel Heath. *Why Indigenous Literatures Matter*. Wilfrid Laurier University Press, 2018.

Kovach, Margaret. *Indigenous Methodologies: Characteristics, Conversations, and Contexts*. University of Toronto Press, 2009.

Lauzon, Jani. "The Search for Spiritual Transformation in Contemporary Theatre Practice." *Performing Indigeneity*, edited by Yvette Nolan and Ric Knowles, Playwrights Canada Press, 2016, pp. 87–97.

MacKenzie, Sarah. *Indigenous Women's Theatre in Canada: A Mechanism of Decolonization*. Fernwood Publishing, 2020.

Nolan, Yvette. *Annie Mae's Movement*. Playwrights Canada Press, 1998 and 2006.

Nolan, Yvette. *Medicine Shows: Indigenous Performance Culture*. Playwrights Canada Press, 2015.

Peters, Charlie. "The Hierarchy on Its Side Becomes a Circle: The Directing Practices and Mentorship of Yvette Nolan." *Theatre Research in Canada*, vol. 44, no. 1, 2023, pp. 14–27.

ROOM Magazine. "Yvette Nolan on Dramaturgy and the Activism of Art: An Interview" *ROOM Magazine*, July 31, 2016. https://roommagazine.com/yvette-nolan-on-dramaturgy-and-the-activism-of-art-an-interview. Accessed December 31, 2023.

Syron, Liza-Mare. *Rehearsal Practices of Indigenous Women Theatre Makers*. Palgrave Macmillan, 2021.

NOTES

1 For more, see Peters.
2 For more on Turtle Gals' work, see Nolan's *Medicine Shows*.

Chapter 8
Agency through Adaptation
MENA Women in *Shakespeare's Sisters, Jogging,* and *Noura*[1]

Nabra Nelson and Marina Johnson

Middle Eastern and North African (MENA) women's bodies have been politicized throughout history, as they exist within a complicated intersection of race, gender, class, and religion. Some important women writers who laid the groundwork for performance we encounter today are Palestinian-born May Ziadeh (1886–1941) who hosted literary salons that focused on feminist thought and writings she called "plays" or "dialogues," and Egyptian playwright Fawziya Mahran (1931–2019) wrote plays like *Al-Buyut* (Homes) critiquing women's treatment in the home and society (Selaiha and Enany 628–636). These women, and other pioneers like them, used political and social moments as a focus in their work. In this chapter, we highlight the ways that Middle Eastern women playwrights, to use Lila Abu-Lughod's term, "write against culture" (138). In this phrase, Abu-Lughod references the literal act of writing against Clifford and Marcus's 1986 anthology, *Writing Culture*, that excluded feminists and people "whose national or cultural identity is mixed by virtue of migration, overseas education, or parentage" (Abu-Lughod 466). By writing against *Western* culture that both homogenizes and excludes, Abu-Lughod solidifies the need to bring people into the conversation whose identities expand and complexify cultural and political discussions. Similar to the way that Ziadeh, Mahran, and other early feminist artists used sociopolitical moments as a starting point for their artistic work and critique, we use September 11, 2001, as our political and historical point of departure. By writing thoughtful,

 DOI: 10.4324/9781003272854-9

nuanced plays in a post-9/11 world, the playwrights we high-light in the plays *Shakespeare's Sisters, Jogging,* and *Noura* are writing after a moment where the image of Arabs and Muslims in the national and international imagination faced a dramatic shift toward negative stereotypes and when "images of oppressed Muslim women became connected to a mission to rescue them from their cultures" (Abu-Lughbod 6–7). In their works, these playwrights resist the homogenization of the idea of "Middle Eastern women," therefore complicating the image that has become prevalent in the West.

Traditionally, most academic writing functions to streamline and expedite how knowledge is conveyed, and as we considered "milestones" in MENA theatre around gender, the performance texts we sought to include—disparate in time, place, location, and original impetus—complicated this traditional approach. Thus, we searched for new case studies to serve as milestones, and we realized this sense of constriction is something against which we constantly struggle in an archive that regularly excludes MENA plays. Some plays are only available in Arabic, others require additional context to be understood outside their country of origin, and some offer still other challenges. This is the nature of our field, and as such, we chose to highlight several plays that excite us as milestones in adaptation by and about women and gender, moving swiftly from the US to Levant and back in a complicated journey. A note on terminology: In this chapter, we use the term **MENA (Middle East and North Africa)** instead of **SWANA (South West Asia and North Africa)**. While there is understandable pushback against the term Middle East, we use it because of the ease of translation from English to Arabic and its common international usage, which we hope makes our work more accessible to readers from the region. We recognize that not all people from this region identify under the MENA umbrella and that these conversations, which have been happening for years, are ongoing.

Adaptation is a powerful tool for women and staging gender in MENA contexts because it allows audiences a way into the narrative that feels familiar and allows them better access to narratives and characters. For these playwrights, it offers a springboard, an opening to respond, and a place to rewrite and adapt for new ways of seeing the complexity of MENA women's gendered experience. Two of our examples, *Medea* and *A Doll's House* have been the subject of many adaptations that seek to bring the original into specific new cultural contexts, especially regarding the role of women. Adapting famous essays like Virginia Woolf's *A Room of One's Own* functions similarly, providing readers a shortcut into a world that may feel unfamiliar to them.

Through the lens of Pietro Floridia and Mirna Sakhleh's *Shakespeare's Sisters*, Hanane Hajj Ali's *Jogging: Theatre in Progress*, and Heather Raffo's *Noura*, we highlight how these playwrights have used well-known Western texts as a springboard for presenting images of MENA women that go beyond stereotypes constructed by a post-9/11 media. We argue that the playwrights, by featuring a widely known text at the core of the narrative, allow the audience an ease of access that primes them for textual and character attributes with which they might be wholly unfamiliar. Each of these texts takes a classic Western story as its base and uses it to provide new ways of thinking about women: *Shakespeare's Sisters* takes inspiration from Virginia Woolf's *A Room of One's Own, Jogging* reinterprets the story of Medea, and *Noura* is a loose adaptation of Henrik Ibsen's *A Doll's House*. But these adaptations go beyond translation. They recontextualize the source material in time and space, essentially changing the storyline without, in some cases, dramatically altering the plot. They imagine what is beyond the classical tale from the viewpoint of under-written or un-written women characters. These case studies span time periods, Euro-American contexts, and media. Moreover, they utilize a literary canon often taught in the United States, which provides a starting point for playwrights to subvert existing paradigms and deepen understandings of MENA, and specifically Arab, womanhood.

MEDIA DEPICTIONS OF MENA CHARACTERS

One need only look at Dr. Jack Shaheen's body of work, succinctly described in his book and documentary *Reel Bad Arabs: How Hollywood Vilifies a People,* to see how film and television provide many examples of Middle Eastern characters written by writers outside the MENA community to harmful ends:

> It's not easy to face the fact that Arab-as-villain images have been around for more than a century, reaching and affecting most of the world's six billion people. From the earliest silent films of the 1880s, damaging portraits have become so prevalent that viewers of film and TV shows demonstrating these stereotypes may come to perceive reel Arabs as real ones. Constantly repeated, these stereotypes manipulate viewers' thoughts and feelings, conditioning them to ratchet up the forces of rage and unreason. And even persecution. (1)

The struggle that Shaheen illuminates persists in film and on stage today. In a 2021 Zoom talk, "A Cultural Conversation," Palestinian-American playwright Betty Shamieh spoke about refusing to give Western audiences the script they want about MENA characters, which often means that her plays go unproduced. She then noted humorously that if she wrote a play about **honor killings**, she would find immediate success on Broadway because of the desire to see MENA pain and sensationalism. This desire for consuming particular MENA narratives is illustrative of Western media's obsession with "trauma porn," which is defined by Black, queer journalist Brittany Johnson as "media that showcases a group's pain and trauma in excessive amounts for the sake of entertainment." Criticism of trauma porn is not new, yet we continue to see it in both media news representations of the Middle East and in storytelling about the MENA region. Lebanese activist Luma Makari points out that the viral sharing of images from the 2020 Beirut blast "don't incite calls for much-needed collective action, or make change" but rather re-traumatize those most impacted and serve as gruesome entertainment for those most distant from the tragedy. These characteristics of trauma porn extend to theatre that graphically depicts traumatic events in the Middle East with an implicit agenda of inviting non-MENA audience members to become voyeurs of the tragedy.

It is imperative to trace this voyeuristic impulse to the Western roots of theatre, particularly as it shapes archetypes for female characters; the ways that these characters have been written have put a neatly packaged portion of identity onto the stage in ways that are understandable to those outside of the culture but limiting. Examples include the ingenue (an overly innocent girl), the shrew (a nagging angry woman), the damsel in distress, the fat friend, the perfect wife, the girl next door, the mother hen, as well as the manic pixie dream girl, who exists to inspire men through her quirkiness. Often plays about MENA women include additional traits that flatten the characters: they either fight with an oppressive society, religion, or man, or are overly sexualized. Some prevalent MENA women-specific tropes include: the devout Muslim woman, the hijabi pressured to remove her **hijab**, the exotic and sensual woman (often a belly dancer), and the oppressed woman who either yearns for the West and its freedoms or is too ignorant to realize her oppression. These tropes, when intersected with race, ethnicity, and gender, beg the question: What does it mean to be a MENA woman onstage? How are playwrights purposefully "writing against culture" to counteract the harmful representation and narratives which have been prevalent in the Western theatre canon for so long?

These tropes pose logistical problems in addition to representational issues. In the case of the trope where a character removes her hijab, a real casting challenge emerges. One of the problems with this trope is that it means no hijabi actress could authentically play that role because she would ultimately have to remove her hijab to make the change occur onstage. David T. Mitchell and Sharon L. Snyder use the term "**narrative prosthesis**" to illustrate the problem with narratives that use disability to signal something "out of place" and a character that potentially needs to be saved (10). While one cannot compare wearing the hijab to a disability, a comparison can be drawn in the "material metaphor" that indicates that the character is a problem to be solved (Syler and Banks 89). In many ways, it seems an attempt to answer Lila Abu-Lughod's question of "Do Muslim Women Need Saving?" with a resounding and disappointing, *yes*! These narratives render the non-hijab-wearing characters as somehow "saving" the hijabi, helping restore "normalcy" to the world and "ridding" the character of external signals of Islamic-ness. Not only is this an unnuanced view into why women choose to wear or remove the hijab but also reflects the lack of roles specifically written for hijabi actors and ignores conversations concerning the casting of actors who wear the hijab. A similar conversation concerns Sikh men who wear turbans. Can these characters only play hijabi women and Sikh men, respectively? How do directors and designers think about these choices? How can they think expansively about making roles available to those who wear material symbols of their faith?

Hanane Hajj Ali, the writer and performer of *Jogging*, is an actor who wears the hijab. Wearing the hijab is not part of Hajj Ali's costume design or part of the script, it is simply something she dons daily. However, it is a choice that is interpreted by an audience. In *Jogging*, she plays a variety of characters, occasionally putting a wig on over her hijab, obscuring it while keeping her head covered. In the introduction to her script, Hajj Ali notes, "Alone on a bare stage, Hanane—woman, wife, and mother—lifts the veil on her identity, becoming an 'unveiled' performer on stage, where personas progressively parade to fit together like Russian dolls." Hajj Ali's choices illustrate the possibilities for playwrights and actors who want to expand the breadth and depth of their representation onstage by allowing for a multiplicity of options.

Jogging and the other case studies featured here focus on the physical and liminal experiences that women have and how those shape the ways they interact with their world. As Katrina Maurer writes, "Women live in the same physical space as the dominant culture but do not live in the same societal space. [...] they are existent but not present, exposed yet overlooked, neither here nor there." The physical and psychological liminality that MENA women navigate is at the heart of many pieces of cultural production.

SHAKESPEARE'S SISTERS

Marina Barham, the producer of the piece and General Manager and Co-Founder of Al-Harah Theatre (which means The Neighborhood, in Arabic) has said that "Palestinian theater functions successfully as a social institution when it works on Palestinian society from within, taking on controversial social issues" (Al-Saber et al. xxiii). *Shakespeare's Sisters* does precisely that. Developed at Al-Harah Theatre in Beit Jala in Occupied Palestine in 2013, the piece began as a drama therapy and research project on Palestinian attitudes towards "single, divorced and widowed women aged over thirty followed by a series of workshops with women" (Varghese 301). While the text was penned by Pietro Floridia, who also directed the piece, the women involved in the process were paramount in its creation. The story centers on Samira, a professor living on her own who has dedicated her life to teaching and research. One night, Nesma, a young dressmaker, appears at Samira's doorstep seeking freedom from her family's traditional expectations. Living together produces chaos, but Samira and Nesma's friendship flourishes. Nesma's dreams and ambitions propel her to create a space inspired by Shakespeare's imaged sister Judith, a space to recharge, regroup, and, if necessary, revolt. Two other actors play ensemble roles as *Shakespeare's Sisters* interrogates the impact of patriarchal structures on women while providing captivating moments of friendship and joy.

The title references a concept detailed in Virginia Woolf's *A Room of One's Own*, which theorized that if Shakespeare had a sister born with equal, if not more, creative talent, his freedom paired with the patriarchal constraints placed on her would have been enough to drive her to suicide. Within the play, "Shakespeare's Sisters" also becomes the name of Samira's home which functions as a women's club; each woman visits the physical space of the house in order to deal with her liminal spaces: finding love after 40, experiencing divorce, and seeking creativity. In addition to the physical space, "Shakespeare's Sisters" becomes a psychological state that the women carry with them, offering support and care

Fig. 8.1 Raeda Ghazaleh, Adeeb Safadi, and Reem Talhami in *Shakespeare's Sisters* at Al Harah Theatre in Palestine, directed by Pietro Floridia. Photo by Yousef AlSharif.

wherever they go. The women form a space of transformation where all who come to the house can walk away finding renewed agency. At the end of the play, however, the physical location is closed due to community pressure, which leaves the question: How will the women proceed?

In "A Stage of One's Own: Gendered Spaces in Palestinian Performance," Gabriel Varghese analyzes the importance of *Shakespeare's Sisters*, noting that it "presents the Palestinian homeplace as a radical counter-space capable of disordering the centre–periphery dialectic" of patriarchal communities and of the Occupation[2] (302). The play's use of Virginia Woolf's work allows it to "draw upon Palestinian and European epistemic practices to articulate its call for women's liberation" but without Euro-Americans leading the conversation (302). Instead, the dialogue stems from *A Room of One's Own* but centers Palestinian women's agency. Varghese notes that, in Palestine, as with other

> anti-colonial movements in other parts of the world ... women have often had to privilege the goal of national

liberation over their own struggles. One way they have attempted to overcome this barrier has been to align the movement for women's empowerment with the national liberation struggle itself. (302)

For Palestinian women, theatre—and specifically *Shakespeare's Sisters*, which also draws from lived experiences—became a tactic to draw attention to their national and personal struggles.

JOGGING: THEATRE IN PROGRESS

In contrast with *Shakespeare's Sisters* which features five characters, Beirut-based actor Hanane Hajj Ali's play *Jogging: Theatre in Progress* reinterprets the ancient Greek tragedy of *Medea* as a one-woman show.[3] Her play features three characters—Hanane, Yvonne, and Zahra—all played by Hajj Ali. The play begins powerfully:

> We would like to inform you that this play is an illegitimate bastard born of sin, where the thoughts of the actress have become like daughters who get pregnant out of wedlock without a care in the world without having to witness or sign a marriage certificate or obtain an official permit from state security. Whoever feels awkward or shy can leave now and return his or her ticket, which is free anyway. (7–8)

Jogging immediately foregrounds societal perceptions of women, signaling to the audience that they have entered into a transgressive space separate from the shame society seemingly mandates around gender expectations. Hajj Ali tells the story through Medea's perspective, bringing humanity, and occasionally comedy, to a gruesome tale.

Written by Euripides in 431 BCE, *Medea* is a classical play that draws from Greek mythology. Abandoned by her husband who marries another woman, Medea is left alone with their two young children. Infuriated by his betrayal, Medea uses her children to kill Jason's new wife (by having them unknowingly poison her) and kills them too. In addition to examining injustice and revenge, *Medea* also subverts expectations around the supposedly inherent maternal nature of women. This ancient text is resonant today as women are frequently relegated to the domestic sphere and painted by society as irrational or evil if they refuse to fit neatly into the role of wife, mother, and daughter. Barbara Barnett's study, "Medea in the Media," examined 250 news reports on maternal infanticide to explore how the journalists presented the case to readers and found that women tended to be portrayed in overly simplistic terms—either as being driven to insanity or being cruel and heartless by nature (411–412). Oppressive structures, such as the patriarchy, were never mentioned, and mental health issues such as postpartum depression were rarely cited. Flawed mothers are often placed into a "mad" or "bad" dichotomy; the first category contains mothers who are "perfect" but mentally ill, and the latter, mothers who are "inept" (417–418). The play, however, shies away from such dichotomies and instead shines a spotlight on the societal pressures associated with motherhood. It hypothesizes Medea's situation as an inevitable result of patriarchal forces in Greek society, which render Medea dependent on her husband, socially and financially vulnerable, and driven to desperate, violent acts.[4]

Using Medea's narrative as an entry point to connect to a more contemporary event, Hajj Ali tells the story of Yvonne, a Lebanese citizen who killed herself and her three daughters with a poisoned fruit salad in 2009. She first imagines Yvonne's murder/suicide note to be the same as Virginia Woolf's, who killed herself when she recognized that her mental illness would overtake her. Virginia Woolf chose to die to free her husband from the hardships to come: "I feel certain I am going mad again. I feel we can't go through another of those terrible times. And I shan't recover this time" (quoted in Oyebode 280). Hajj Ali quickly notes, though, that imagining Yvonne's suicide note in this manner dismisses the idea that such an act could happen anywhere to anyone. Onstage, after revealing that the suicide note that she read was not that of Yvonne, Hajj Ali adds, "What Woolf said in that letter is what many people imagined Yvonne had said in hers. They said certainly something like that can't happen in our town.

It must be the illness" (17). While Yvonne's story was specific to her, it also relates to women across space and time.

Through the rest of the play, Hajj Ali contextualizes Medea's story with stories from Lebanon, revealing aspects of the interior lives of contemporary Lebanese women who have been made invisible. The narratives raise questions including: What could lead a modern-day Lebanese woman to commit murder or suicide? Do the terms 'murder' and 'suicide' accurately characterize these acts if they are compelled by oppressive systems? How are the nation-state and its infrastructures complicit in these acts of gendered self-sacrifice? But these sacrifices do not usually occur the way they do in *Medea*. As the character in *Jogging* says, "A mother could not kill her children like that no matter what Euripides and the gods who made him say" (15). Though directly after this proclamation, she shares that she grappled with wishing her seven-year-old son would die to end his suffering when he had cancer. Indeed, this is a heartbreaking and complex parallel between the stories that also reveals the social pressures of womanhood and expectations of motherhood.

Hajj Ali worked on *Jogging* for over five years, integrating complex sound, lights, projections, and different theatrical forms. She did not get permission from the Lebanese government to produce her play in 2016, so she could not perform it within any traditional theatre venues. Defying the expectations and artistic process put forth by the government, she crafted the play for alternate spaces with minimal technical elements. While the play usually occurred in theatre-like or multipurpose areas, as the **Arab Spring** was starting, she began to hold performance events in the streets of Beirut.[5] Her street-based performance events often took the form of community-engaged protests—political street theatre that engaged the public, including bystanders, passersby, and sometimes people on their balconies, in dialogue. Her performance of gender actively reflected ongoing political issues while her engagement with the community put the play's subtitle "Theatre in Progress" at the fore—highlighting that progress can only come from the people. From 2016 to 2019, Hajj Ali performed *Jogging* more than one hundred times throughout Lebanon, and has toured the production internationally, receiving accolades such as the Gilder/Coigney International Theatre Award. In Hajj Ali's words,

> Thanks to the revolution, Beirut has become the theatre venue I had always hoped for, one that is as big as the city itself … the original role of the agora of theatre when it was created … to really put on stage among citizens critical issues and to discuss them" (*Jogging* 14:08–14:14; *My Conversation with Lebanese Artist Hanane Hajj Ali* 17:35–17:50)

In seeking a physical space for the citizens of Beirut to be together, Hajj Ali turned the liminal spaces of transit in Beirut into areas that allowed audience members access to the interiority of her characters. By staging women's stories in the street, Hajj Ali not only highlighted the stories themselves, she also highlighted the idea that women's stories are continually in progress, being told, retold, and redefined through history. Oppressive patriarchal structures in society and politics are threads connecting disparate moments and places in the lives and history of women. Staging these stories makes these threads visible and puts the power in the hands of the women to tell their stories in progress.

NOURA

Iraqi-American playwright and performer Heather Raffo's 2018 play *Noura* is an adaptation of Henrik Ibsen's *A Doll's House*, a play that also often raises debate regarding early modernist discussions of gender roles. In Raffo's text, Noura and her husband Tariq are Christian Iraqi refugees to the United States. With their best friend and their son, they prepare to celebrate Christmas; Noura clings to the traditions from home while grappling with her family's increasingly Western identity. Maryam, a college-aged recent refugee from Mosul, comes to spend Christmas with the family, not knowing the secret that connects Noura and herself, a detail that, in fact, is known only to Noura. Secrets are revealed, identities are unraveled, and the family questions how their desire to assimilate into United States culture impacts their relationships with each other and the world around them.

Though both born in Mosul, Noura and Maryam live different embodied realities of what it means to be an Iraqi woman. When and how they fled the war, combined with the generational gap between them and the ways they each internalized societal norms around gender and shame, divide them. Maryam's decision to become pregnant out of wedlock confuses Noura, who finds this approach to motherhood untraditional, shocking, and potentially shackling, especially for women born in an Iraqi context. For Maryam, however, the construct of the "traditional" family has been weaponized to control women: "I never had a father. I'm what everyone's afraid of, a woman without a guardian. I'm unrestrainable" (Raffo 80). Maryam is highly independent and exercises agency over her life in ways that Noura never saw as a possibility which creates feelings of shame and jealousy that paint a complicated picture of what it means to be a wife, mother, friend, immigrant, Christian, and woman.

The title character in Raffo's play—Noura—borrows her name from the protagonist in Norwegian playwright Henrik Ibsen's *A Doll's House*—Nora. Though Ibsen did not see himself as addressing the "woman question" in his play, a play featuring a woman who leaves her oppressive husband was quite progressive when first performed in Copenhagen, Denmark, in 1879 (Templeton 28). In Ibsen's play, Nora seems content playing the roles of wife, mother, and homemaker. Her husband teases her about the habits from which she derives pleasure and agency, like treating herself to small snacks. He views her as an object, using infantilizing nicknames for her like "skylark," "squirrel," and "doll" (Ibsen 95). Despite her husband's infantilizing treatment, Nora makes a financial choice to aid her family that places her and her family in jeopardy. This conflict forces her to take control of her life in ways she was not socialized to do, and for which she has no women role models. By the end of the play, she goes from being a submissive wife and mother into an independent woman who decides to leave her three children and home to find herself. The last sound of the play is a door slam as she leaves, what drama critic James Gibbons Huneker famously called the "slammed door (which) reverberated across the roof of the world" (quoted in Buitenhuis 83).

Fig. 8.2 Moogie Fawaz, Amanda Najor, Heather Raffo, and Kal Naga in *Noura* at Detroit Public Theatre, Detroit, MI, directed by Mike Mosallam. Photo by Alex Lumelsky.

Nora's choice to leave her husband and her children caused a stir, especially in 1879. Audiences and critics were not sure what to make of Nora, Torvald, or even Ibsen (Templeton 29–32). In 1889, the *Daily News* critiqued the play as unrealistic, positing that no woman could be as selfish as to leave her husband and children merely because her husband was "angry" with her (Egan 103). *A Doll's House* questioned the institution of marriage and, by extension, the patriarchy and gendered power dynamics across society. Ibsen's contemporary, playwright August Strindberg, said in 1884, of *A Doll's House,* "Marriage was revealed as being a far from divine institution, people stopped regarding it as an automatic provider of absolute bliss, and divorce between incompatible parties came at last to be accepted as conceivably justifiable" (quoted in Ibsen 17).

Just as Ibsen's *A Doll House* illuminated relevant gendered social issues such as marriage, motherhood, and women's social and financial autonomy, so too does *Noura*. According to Raffo, *Noura*

> is not unrelated to the ever-present question I heard talking about in my Brooklyn parenting circles, can women be fully realized in all of their roles? Can they belong equally in each? Or is it inevitable that having a career, being a wife, a mother, a daughter, perhaps to aging parents, that one of these roles will become unsustainable? In the demand of playing roles for so many others is it inevitable that we question who we really are ourselves? (iv)

In addition to questioning social constructs of and expectations around women's roles more broadly, Heather Raffo also expressed her exhaustion at living in a theatre landscape that holds Nora up as a "beacon of feminist thought" (iii). Raffo did not see herself, on multiple levels, represented in Ibsen's *A Doll's House,* yet she realized that "a different conflict between individualism and community was playing out before [her] eyes, not just as an Arab American, but also as a modern wife and mother" (iii).

CONCLUSION

The women in *Shakespeare's Sisters, Jogging,* and *Noura* were all written "against culture" as their playwrights explored their intersectional identities through the vehicle of adaptation. The idea of these MENA women playwrights taking a Western classic text as a reference point from which to create new, complicated women characters might seem counterintuitive, as though it centers the West. However, we argue that the playwrights re-center the stories in the Middle East, and utilize these known narratives to create a shorthand to make the characters more accessible to broader audiences which then offers avenues to complicate depictions of MENA characters and women. Whether they are MENA characters being represented on stages in the United States more expansively for the first time, or characters who spark a dialogue within their communities in Lebanon or Palestine, the playwrights' refusal to homogenize MENA women opens new avenues for representation that have shifted and continue to shape the theatre landscape.

FURTHER RESOURCES

Chandler, Clare. "'Let Me Be Part of the Narrative'—The Schuyler Sisters 'Almost' Feminist?" *Contemporary Theatre Review*, April 17, 2020. http://www.contemporarytheatrereview.org/2018/ chandler-hamilton-almost-feminist/. Accessed June 15, 2023.
This article analyzes the prominent Broadway show *Hamilton* through an intersectional feminist lens, considering issues of race and gender in critiquing the famously color-consciously cast show.

Denyer, Heather. "Heather Raffo on *Noura*." *Arab Stages*, 2016. https://arabstages.org/2016/10/heather-raffo-on-noura/. Accessed January 29, 2023.
This article about Heather Raffo's *Noura* is one example of the content you will find in the online, peer-reviewed theatre journal *Arab Stages*.

Johnson, Marina, and Nabra Nelson, co-hosts. *Kunafa and Shay* podcast, HowlRound Theatre Commons. http://howlround.com/ series/kunafa-and-shay. Accessed August 20, 2023.
Named for sweets (kunafa) and tea (shay) that offer space for conversation, this podcast series considers modern/contemporary MENA theatre through interviews with artists and discussions of global community-engaged works.

Khoury, Jamil. "American Swana: A Progressive Theatre Movement Soars." *American SWANA: A Progressive Theatre Movement Soars | Mass Review*, February 12, 2021. http://massreview.org/ node/10720. Accessed February 14, 2021.
Founding Co-Executive Artistic Director of Silk Road Rising, Jamil Khoury, shares the status of MENA/SWANA coalition-building in the US, including the origins of MENATMA, and considers the terms MENA and SWANA in-depth.

"MENA Theatre Makers Alliance About." *MENA Theatre Makers Alliance.* http://www.menatheatre.org/. Accessed July 14, 2023.
MENATMA is the US coalition for MENA theatre-makers. Their mission statement reads: "MENA Theater Makers Alliance amplifies the voices of Middle Eastern and North African theater makers and expands how stories from and about our communities are told on US stages. We will take space, make opportunities, champion artists, and build relationships with other marginalized communities and allies to build a more vibrant American theater."

Raffo, Heather. *Heather Raffo's Iraq Plays: The Things That Can't Be Said: 9 Parts of Desire; Fallujah; Noura*. Methuen Drama, 2021.

You can find more of Heather Raffo's plays in this anthology, including her one-person show *Nine Parts of Desire* and *Fallujah*, the first opera about the Iraq War.

Sawaf, Kholoud. *10,000 Balconies.*

Set in modern Syria and loosely inspired by *Romeo and Juliet*, this play is currently unpublished but definitely worth locating. For production information visit: https://www.theatre2. org/balconies?gad=1&gclid=Cj0KCQjwi7GnBhDXARIsAFLvH 4lTPlKQPkAsmjKhk7_-ZFpWJDMDHiv-Bj9AxDGT-WnTY GyPHZqj4kEaAj5AEALw_wcB. Accessed September 5, 2022.

Yeghiazarian, Torange, and Jamil Khoury. "A Middle Eastern American Theatre Artists Bill of Rights." https://goldenthread. org/about/bill-of-rights/. Accessed July 10, 2023.

Written by the former Artistic Director of Golden Thread Productions and the Founding Co-Executive Artistic Director of Silk Road Rising, this document outlines self-stated rights of MENA theatre-makers in the US.

REFERENCES

Abu-Lughod, Lila. *Do Muslim Women Need Saving?* Harvard University Press, 2015.

Al-Saber, Samer, et al. "Shakespeare's Sisters." *Stories Under Occupation: And Other Plays from Palestine*. Seagull Books, 2020, pp. 109–148.

Barnett, Barbara. "Medea in the Media: Narrative and Myth in Newspaper Coverage of women who kill their children." *Journalism*, vol. 7, no. 4, 2006, pp. 411–432.

Buitenhuis, Peter. "After the Slam of A Doll's House Door: Reverberations in the Work of James, Hardy, Ford and Wells." *Mosaic: An Interdisciplinary Critical Journal*, vol. 17, no. 1, 1984, pp. 83–96.

Egan, Michael. *Henrik Ibsen: The Critical Heritage*. Routledge, 1997.

Hajj Ali, Hanane. *Jogging: Theatre in Progress*, 2018.

Hajj Ali, Hanane, Hanane Hajj Ali on *"Jogging—Theatre in Progress,"* Berliner Festspiele, May 14, 2018. https://www.youtube.com/ watch?v=dFK1EtjWTA0. Accessed August 28, 2023.

Huneker, James. *Iconoclasts: A Book of Dramatists*. Charles Scribner's Sons, 1905.

Ibsen, Henrik. *Ibsen Plays: 2: A Doll's House; an Enemy of the People; Hedda Gabler*. Bloomsbury Methuen Drama, 2014.

"'Jogging' by Hanane Hajj Ali, Winner of 2020 Gilder/Coigney Int'l Theatre Award YouTube Video." Performance by Hanane Hajj Ali, YouTube, League of Professional Theatre Women, March 8, 2021. https://www.youtube.com/watch?v=UCdp0W UF5ag. Accessed July 14, 2023.

Johnson, Brittany. "What Is Trauma Porn?" *The Mighty*, June 22, 2023. https://themighty.com/topic/mental-health/trauma-porn. Accessed July 14, 2023.

Makari, Luma. "Trauma Porn and the Commodification of Lebanon's Tragedy." *The New Humanitarian*, November 8, 2022. http://www.thenewhumanitarian.org/opinion/first-person/2022/1/25/trauma-porn-commodification-of-Lebanon-tragedy. Accessed February 5, 2021.

Maurer, Katrina. "Living in the Liminal: A Contemporary Feminist's Experience Living in the in-Between." November 24, 2014. fempopculture.blogspot.com/2014/11/living-in-liminal-contemporary.html. Accessed July 14, 2023.

Mitchell, David T., and Sharon L. Snyder. *Narrative Prosthesis: Disability and the Dependencies of Discourse*. University of Michigan Press, 2011.

My Conversation with Lebanese Artist Hanane Hajj Ali, Jogging, Ahmed Tharwat, February 3, 2020. https://www.youtube.com/watch?v=V5PQtCn81ao. Accessed August 28, 2023.

Oyebode, Femi. "'Dearest, I Feel Certain I Am Going Mad Again': The Suicide Note of Virginia Woolf." *Advances in Psychiatric Treatment*, vol. 16, no. 4, July 2010, pp. 280. https://doi.org/10.1192/apt.16.4.280.

Raffo, Heather. *Noura*. Samuel French, 2019.

Selaiha, Nehad, and Sarah Enany. "Women Playwrights in Egypt." *Theatre Journal*, vol. 62, no. 4, December 2010, pp. 627–643.

Shaheen, Jack G. *Reel Bad Arabs: How Hollywood Vilifies a People*. Olive Branch Press, 2010.

Shamieh, Betty, and Lou Hamou-Lhad. "A Cultural Conversation: Betty Shamieh & Lou Hamou-Lhadj," Lecture at Stanford University, moderated by Dr. Samer Al-Saber Shamieh, Zoom, Stanford University, April 29, 2021.

Syler, Claire, and Daniel Banks. *Casting a Movement: The Welcome Table Initiative*. Routledge, 2019.

Templeton, Joan. "The 'Doll House' Backlash: Criticism, Feminism, and Ibsen." *PMLA/Publications of the Modern Language Association of America*, vol. 104, no. 1, 1989, pp. 28–40. https://doi.org/10.2307/462329.

Varghese, Gabriel. "A Stage of One's Own: Gendered Spaces in Palestinian Performance." *Studies in Theatre and Performance*, vol. 37, no. 3, 2016, pp. 301–315. https://doi.org/10.1080/14682761.2016.1185682.

NOTES

1 This article was adapted from the authors' *Kunafa and Shay* podcast episode "Complicating Notions of Womanhood" (Season 1, Episode 7) produced by HowlRound Theatre Commons. We are

grateful to Christine Xiong, Suhaila Meera, and Vineet Gupta for their feedback on early drafts of this chapter.

2 In this instance, Occupation is defined as military control by a ruling power, in this case Israel, over a country, Palestine, that is outside their geographic confines.

3 We had the privilege of reading the unpublished English script with Hajj Ali's permission.

4 Given the ways that *Medea* critiques sociocultural pressures on women, many recent adaptations of *Medea* center on immigration, highlighting the gendered effects of cultural clashes in migration and the diaspora such as Luis Alfaro's *Medea in Los Angeles*.

5 The Arab Spring was a series of anti-government protests that took place across much of the Arab world beginning in late 2010 and continuing for several years. Beginning in Tunisia, it then spread to Libya, Egypt, Yemen, Syria, and Bahrain, with additional protests and demonstrations occurring in other countries.

Chapter 9

Staging and Critiquing Masculinities

Between Pancho Villa and a Naked Woman and *Straight White Men*

Ramón Esquivel

What about men and masculinities? In a text about staging genders and sexualities, it seems apt and necessary to consider how artists and dramatists consider and perform masculinities. To not do so would suggest masculinities are not gender expressions, in fact often existing as the standard against which other gender expressions are defined. Barrett and Whitehead define *masculinities* as "behaviors, languages and practices, existing in specific cultural and organizational locations, which are commonly associated with men, thus culturally defined as not feminine" (15–16). Gender scholar Judith Butler offers, "Gender proves to be performance—that is, constituting the identity it is purported to be. In this sense, gender is always a doing, though not a doing by a subject who might be said to pre-exist the dead" (25). While other chapters reference masculinity and consider its performance in various contexts, this chapter specifically focuses on masculinity and examines the ways performance can illuminate the complexities of masculinity, the socialized performance of masculinity, and the patriarchy.

In theatre, men have often written and produced plays that center men, especially those with conventional expressions of masculinities. Men have written about and critiqued masculinities in their plays, such as Arthur Miller's *Death of a*

DOI: 10.4324/9781003272854-10

Salesman, August Wilson's *Fences*, Sam Shepard's *True West*, David Mamet's *Glengarry Glen Ross*, and Luis Valdez's *Zoot Suit*. In these examples and others, the dramatic conflict is rooted in men wrestling with rigid notions of masculinity. While other characters may face consequences of men's actions, especially women and children, these plays are primarily interested in how the men are affected.

Of course, there have also been notable, lauded examples of men writing plays that center women characters. Federico Garcia Lorca's *The House of Bernarda Alba: A Drama of Women in the Villages of Spain* (1936), is the story of a matriarch and her five daughters. Tennessee Williams gave us Amanda Wingfield in *The Glass Menagerie* (1944) and Blanche DuBois in *A Streetcar Named Desire* (1947). Winnie, buried up to her waist, dominates Samuel Beckett's *Happy Days* (1961). *Agnes of God* (1979) by John Pielmeier has three women characters: two nuns and a psychiatrist. Robert Harling's *Steel Magnolias* (1987) is about Southern women. Edward Albee won the Pulitzer Prize for Drama for *Three Tall Women* (1991), in which the only man in the play does not speak. Though these plays center women, their dramatic tensions are often rooted in conflicts with or caused by men, whether the men appear on stage or not. These plays also reflect how patriarchy has historically privileged men playwrights and actors in depicting women on stage.

In the United States, 35 women playwrights as of 2023 have had their plays produced on Broadway (Bien). While many have, understandably, centered women characters in their stories, others broke through with stories about men. Lorraine Hansberry's *A Raisin the Sun* (1959) features three dynamic women in Lena, Ruth, and Beneatha Younger, but their lives and futures are determined by the whims of the man of the house, Walter. Suzan-Lori Parks won the Pulitzer Prize for Drama for her play about brothers, Lincoln and Booth, in *Topdog/Underdog* (2001), and examined the complexities of Black masculinity in the US. French dramatist Yasmina Reza wrote about three men talking about *Art* and navigating their friendship (2007), while Katori Hall explored the humanity of Dr. Martin Luther King, Jr. in *The Mountaintop* (2011).

By writing and foregrounding male characters, Hansberry, Parks, Reza, and Hall explore intersections of race, class, and gender within US contexts in their work, while also challenging the assumption that women can only write and understand other women.

Also writing across identities are Young Jean Lee and Sabina Berman, who examine power and privilege in the US and Mexico, respectively. Young Jean Lee's work explores identity politics related to Asian Americans, Black Americans, and women in plays like *Untitled Feminist Show* (2011) and *Songs of the Dragon Flying to Heaven* (2006). She became the first Asian-American woman to open a play on Broadway with *Straight White Men* in 2018. As one of Mexico's most prominent female playwrights, Sabina Berman's works focus on gender, power, identity, and politics. Her play *Entre Villa y una mujer desnuda (Between Pancho Villa and a Naked Woman)* was a hit in Mexico in 1993, and made into a 1996 film, co-directed by Berman. In *Straight White Men* and *Between Pancho Villa and a Naked Woman,* Lee and Berman are key voices in presenting masculinities not as default or neutral gender expressions but as a set of distinct, observable, and chosen behaviors.

To reinforce the idea that we are watching men "doing" masculinity, Lee and Berman tell their stories through the lenses of women, transgender, and nonbinary persons. In *Between Pancho Villa and a Naked Woman*, Berman makes Gina and then Paulina the point-of-view characters, or the characters through whom the audience views the action and world of the play. Further complicating, expanding, and contrasting binaristic ideas of gender and heterosexual masculinity, Lee employs the Persons in Charge 1 and 2 to flip and heighten the gender dynamics and the audience's awareness of them. In the notes for *Straight White Men*, she writes "Ideally, Person in Charge 1 and Person in Charge 2 should be played by transgender or non-binary performers (preferably of color)" (8). The *Straight White Men* of the title are then beholden to the narrative control and staging of these Persons. The Persons in Charge facilitate scene changes and even place characters at the start of scenes, posing them, as if in a dollhouse. At the start of the play, they interact with the audience, answering their questions and addressing any complaints—all underscoring that the audience is watching a play performed by actors working from a script written by a woman. This establishes a frame for the play; the audience is watching characters through the lens of sexual orientation, race, and gender identities, and it is all a performance. As such, it brings into question the notion of masculinity being the standard position. According to Person in Charge 2, "Living in Western culture, I'm supposed to wanna be a straight man" (11). Framing the story this way invites audiences to consider if the lives presented on stage are truly ideal. The straight white men who are supposed to represent the center of privileged power in Western society do not seem happy themselves, which has harmful consequences for everyone.

"DOING" MASCULINITIES: COMPETITION AND DOMINATION

Competition and establishing dominance motivate characters in *Straight White Men* and *Between Pancho Villa and a Naked Woman*. These men compete in intellectualized environments like universities, book publishing, and nonprofit organizations instead of battlefields, sports arenas, or other spaces of physical competition. Their ideas of usefulness and legacy are rooted in competition. Their work and, more importantly, being recognized for it financially, publicly, socially, and/or politically means that a man is "winning" in the game of life. He gains dominance and additional power within the patriarchy and other accompanying structures like capitalism. Even awareness of male privilege is presented as a tactic for elevating oneself above other men.

In *Straight White Men*, Jake and Drew try to make sense of their oldest brother Matt's decision to settle into a life of companionship and assistance for their widower father, Ed, as well as Matt's comfort with his job as a clerical worker for a local nonprofit organization. Despite Ed's comment that he hasn't "seen him this cheerful in years," Jake and Drew are concerned about their brother (Lee 44). The brothers have competed their whole lives in games, academics, and social life, all of which Matt usually won, proving himself to be the example of a well-intentioned yet clearly powerful, traditionally masculine man. Drew relates a story of Matt's response to a crude game that Jake and his friends played:

> Do you know about when Matt pissed on Jake's friends? [...] Matt got mad because Jake and his friends were playing "Gay Chicken." [...] It's where straight guys dare each other to do shit like, I don't know, put their balls on each other's faces, and whoever chickens out first, loses [...] Anyway, Matt of course found this to be totally offensive, so he asked if he could play, took out his dick, and pissed all over Jake and his friends! (30)

Matt had a reputation for championing progressive causes since his youth, but he also had the capacity to dominate his brothers and other men, often in an animalistic, equally crude way, when he chose to do so. Jake, Drew, and Ed believe he still has this capacity, and they are baffled why he chooses not to tap into it. Though he never quite articulates it, Matt has chosen to stop "doing" masculinity. While he seems content about it, his choice also triggers a crisis of masculinity for his brothers and, eventually, his father.

Jake has internalized a rigid idea of doing masculinity by dominating others, so he tries to understand Matt's life in the context of competition. A banker, Jake acts selfishly, makes jokes at others' expense, and is materialistic. He is the stereotype of a privileged, straight, white man, and he owns it:

> Look at me! I'm an asshole, but people kind of like me, whether they know it or not [...] I give my friends shit for acting "gay." I joke about which interns I want to fuck [...] All day long, I reinforce a system that keeps us on top. (67)

Articulating his privilege is less introspection and more rhetoric, however, as Jake has no intention to change. To make sense of Matt's choice within a rigid idea of masculinity, Jake believes that Matt is intentionally giving up his privilege as a straight white man so that others can step into roles that he would have occupied, and in so doing, he is manipulating his way to "winning," an act still within the guise of traditional, rigid, binaristic masculinity:

> All our lives, guys like us have been told to get out of the way so that other people can have a chance. Matt's actually doing what they want! It's noble! [...] You just don't feel noble because no one appreciates it. All your minority coworkers are probably too busy with their ambition to notice you're there. (67)

Who are the "other people?" Jake implies that anyone who is not a straight white man like his father, brothers, and himself are forcing them out of positions of power and tearing down the system that has been keeping them "on top." He reasons that if everyone wants straight white men to vanish, Matt is giving them what they want. Convincing Matt that this is his motivation means Jake and his worldview wins—a further testament to Jake's success within the competition of patriarchal society.

Drew also sees Matt's life through the lens of competition, but he believes his brother is "losing" because he is depressed

Fig. 9.1 Austin Pendleton, Gary Wilmes, Pete Simpson, James Stanley in *Straight White Men*, 2014. Photo by Blaine Davis.

and unable to assume the kind of life that someone of his privileged status should and is expected to occupy. Fluent in the language of emotional intelligence, Drew uses vulnerability as a tactic. He discusses his history of mental illness openly and shares the benefits of therapy.

> I wasn't really living. So then Mom died ... and I went to see a therapist, and my whole fucking life started to change. Every good thing that's happened to me has happened since then! Matt, please just give it a shot! (70)

At the same time, Drew refuses to listen to Matt, or consider that his own interpretation could be wrong. He threatens to end his relationship with Matt when Matt demurs on the idea of going to therapy:

> Matt, you gotta help me out here. I'm not gonna watch you destroy your life. I've been enabling you for too long. I'm not gonna do it. If you won't agree to make some honest attempt to improve your life, I'm done, man. I can't have any more contact with you [...] Just promise me you're gonna take one positive step. I'll do everything in my power to help you. (70)

Drew uses the language of vulnerability to *sound* like he cares about Matt, but his ultimatum suggests that he is only trying to win a debate.

If Lee aims to understand and critique the competition of manhood among straight white men, in *Between Pancho Villa and a Naked Woman*, Sabina Berman addresses **machismo**, "a social behavior pattern in which the Latino male exhibits an overbearing attitude to anyone in a position he perceives as inferior to his, demanding complete subservience" (Mendoza 1). In the play, Alberto expresses masculine dominance in a different way. His domain is in writing and teaching—a profession often historically associated with women and femininity. Being a man of letters may not command the same respect as a military general like Pancho Villa, a famous leader of the Mexican Revolution, and because of this, Alberto distinguishes his style as more masculine: "I'm not striving for linguistic finesse. My book won't be written with a limp wrist. I want people to feel the violence of the situation: I want my book to smell of horses, of sweat, of gunpowder" (Berman 22). Alberto implies that describing the battles is as valorous as participating in them, celebrating violence, power, and heterosexuality. He sees himself as a soldier in the revolution by proxy; his words are his bullets. In fact, Alberto draws his book in the same fashion that Villa draws his pistol. Alberto is convinced that his work is as important—and as masculine—as Villa's. By placing the book-wielder and pistol-bearer side by side, Berman sets this "doing" of *machismo* up for a laugh in its comparison.

Alberto also regards his relationship with Gina as a competition. Advised by the historical Pancho Villa, the subject of his book, Alberto is torn between two strategies for relating to Gina: negotiate the boundaries of their relationship or bend her will to his. The dual scene with Alberto in bed with Gina, and Villa visiting with the Woman, links the men's fates. Alberto admires the way Villa toys with the Woman: "He just pretended to sip [the tea]; he was just buying a little more time" (31–32). When Villa shoots the Woman, the violence is jarring, sudden, and cruel, but Alberto admires the decisiveness of the action. When Gina, at the turning point in the play, asserts herself by communicating her desire to live with Alberto and have a child, he plays it cool, like Villa did with the Woman, and agrees. Alberto sees this as a tactic to gain control, and he then suddenly vanishes for several months.

However, in these attempts at asserting masculinity/machismo are confounded by independent, empowered women. Gina's response to Alberto's disappearance shows that his attempt to gain power backfired; she sees this action as cowardice. Gina's certainty and independence threaten Alberto, who, trying to gain control, denigrates her womanhood:

> Ours was a beautiful relationship based on lust, but you had to let yourself get carried away by the female urge to nest. You had to turn our passion into a matter of shared bathrooms and baby bottles and dry-cleaning bills. You had to trap me here in your home, you had to conduct yourself like a "woman." (97)

Pancho Villa, too, is confounded by an empowered woman. He suggests that Alberto kill Gina, just as Villa shot the Woman. Instead, Alberto attempts to kill himself by jumping out the window, and in a fitting final moment with Gina, he humiliates himself because she lives on the first floor (99). Of course, Alberto has more options besides murder and suicide, and a rational, respectful response would have been for Alberto to accept Gina's decision and walk out the front door. But he is unable to break his rigid idea of *machismo*. In his socialized view of manhood, also reinforced by history as symbolized by Villa, Alberto is no man if he is unable to bring Gina to heel, and he sees death as his only option, unsuccessful as it is.

Isaac presents an alternative to Alberto's toxic, aggressive *machismo*. He asks Gina to move in with him. He puts Gina's happiness first because he genuinely cares for her. Isaac never competes with Alberto, even if he is appalled by Alberto's treatment of Gina. Unlike Alberto, Isaac doesn't see Gina as a prize to be won. When Gina leads Isaac in the bolero, he lets her, and he is even turned on by her leading (65). Alberto could do this as well but to do so would threaten his deeply held and socialized sense of masculinity, dependent on power, dominance, and control.

Both plays present multiple ways to express and embody masculinities while also satirically pointing to the complexities associated with them and the sociocultural contexts that shape them. Patriarchy is so pervasive that it is invisible to the characters, yet they perform their patriarchal roles and socially inscribed masculinities fully. Often justified by the phrase "boys will be boys," patriarchy contorts the gender spectrum into a wheel with masculinities at the center, and all other gender expressions radiating out from it. However, if we reframe and reconsider this wheel as a spectrum, masculinity becomes but one of many gender expressions, perhaps even containing many different forms of masculinities. Whitehead and Barrett write:

> Men have much to gain, not least in achieving emotional well-being, empathy with others, quality of relationships, reflexivity, and balance in their lives. For the sake of this

and future generations it can only be good that men recognize they have a gender, rather than perceive gender o
be about women and, thus, peripheral to how they experience the world. (3–4)

This reframing seems essential for achieving justice for those
of other gender expressions, and it serves men, too, for they,
like some characters in Lee and Berman's plays, will see that
the incoherent and impossible expectations they have internalized are merely constructs.

"DOING" MASCULINITIES: TACTICAL LANGUAGE

The men in these plays have internalized rigid ideas of performing masculinities, which, as gender is socially constructed,
are reinforced by "audiences" within each story world. They
are sensitive to how others hear their words and perceive their
actions, and that social pressure (real or imagined) to "do"
masculinity acts as a corrective. Lee and Berman write the men
not as overtly chauvinist pigs, raving bigots, or vicious homo-
phobes, but as middle-class liberals, fluent in the language of
diversity, equity, and inclusion, and aware of their privilege.
Matt, Jake, and Drew even grew up playing Privilege, which
their mother made by modifying a Monopoly game. As Ed
says, "Well how else were you gonna learn not to be assholes?"
(Lee 19). But the brothers, like Alberto, interpret "not being
an asshole" as a tactic for improving how one is perceived,
not about respecting others. In this context, respecting women
and treating them as equals is more about being *seen* as more
enlightened than other men, and therefore is more attractive.
These factors are important to understanding how language
figures into the performative nature of masculinities.

Trying to win Gina back, Alberto appeals to her understanding of how men are shaped by *machismo*. Acknowledging that
he has hurt her has worked to lower Gina's guard before, so he
tries again after returning from spending months in Toronto:
"I'm irresponsible. I abandon what I love most. I don't know
why […] you want to change me. It would be better to trade
me for another man" (Berman 23–24). Alberto believes that

Gina will see his admission of fault as virtue, though he has no inclination to change his behavior. It is a tactic to get Gina to see him as a wounded man who is powerless to resist temptation. Although *machismo* encourages a man to have many women lovers, **marianismo,** the feminine counterpart to *machismo*, requires a woman to remain a virgin until married and to engage in sexual intercourse solely for the purpose of procreation (Ceballos 1). This gives the virginal woman moral superiority over the promiscuous man. In this context, Alberto suggesting that he does not deserve Gina is a specific tactic used to give her the illusion of power in their relationship.

In the dramatic climax of *Between Pancho Villa and a Naked Woman*, Alberto makes a show of being magnanimous towards Gina. He "accepts" that Gina is with Isaac, and he *allows* her to continue to see him (Berman 84). For the *macho*, the willingness to share his woman with another man would be considered extraordinarily generous and permissive. Alberto accepts Gina's relationship with Isaac to give Gina the illusion of equality between them. When Gina tells him no, Alberto refuses to accept her answer: "You can't. You can't. I won't let you. You can't" (93). Villa implores Alberto to kill Gina to reassert his manhood, but the only weapon Alberto has is a copy of his new book, which he takes out "like a revolver" (94). The humor of the moment belies its danger; Alberto wishes to kill Gina. In a patriarchal system, challenging a man's masculinity is an offense punishable by death.

For Alberto, divergence from traditional *machismo* behavior causes tension, triggering the appearance of Pancho Villa. As a storytelling device, the presence of the revolutionary war hero externalizes Alberto's internal struggle. His words and actions towards Gina seem penitent and desperate but they are ultimately performative. Villa's advice reveals darker, manipulative motivations. Villa is the ultimate macho Mexican man in Alberto's eyes, and his advice and chastising reflect the power of *machismo*. To Villa, Alberto facing off with Gina is a matter of life and death. Villa's own interactions with the Woman and his mother—played by the same actor as Gina when she imagines the scene from Alberto's book (41)—give background into his mindset. He assumed the Woman was trying to poison him, and he assumed his mother wanted him to give up the revolution to stay with her. Both actions would have killed him in their own ways, and both require relinquishing power to a woman.

For Alberto, Pancho Villa is a constant reminder of what he must do to prove himself a true, powerful Mexican man. His visions of Villa become more vivid, judgmental, and aggressive as Alberto realizes he has no "leverage" over Gina (85). Villa coaxes Alberto into wooing Gina into submission with calculated language rooted in *machismo:*

VILLA. She's just another woman, *compañero.* You'll go and she'll stay standing beside this door forever, like a statue. She'll stay closed in her own little world and you'll find other welcoming arms—there's never any shortage of those. Younger arms. Softer ones. More innocent eyes.

ALBERTO. Gina ... you're the last woman I'll ever love ...

VILLA. *Andale.* We may be wounded but we're not dead yet. (91)

When Gina is unmoved, Alberto becomes hysterical. His earlier acceptance ends, and he pivots to more authoritarian words. "You can't do this to me. Not to me ... You can't. You can't. I won't let you. You can't" (93). In a final act of magnanimity, what he considers his most generous gesture of love, Alberto relents and agrees to get divorced (98). At that point, Gina sees through him. Her laughter drives him to desperation, and the threat of violence that has been building through the scene reaches its peak.

Berman's use of Pancho Villa as Alberto's alter ego and internal voice is like the relationship between El Pachuco and Henry Reyna in Luis Valdez's play *Zoot Suit* (1978). Based on actual events in Los Angeles in the 1940s, *Zoot Suit's* Reyna chooses to leave the East Los Angeles gang that he has led and his *pachuco* lifestyle to enlist in the U.S. Navy during World War II. When Reyna and his friends are falsely accused of murder and subjected to a prejudiced legal system, he questions the wisdom of choosing a path deemed more respectable by his parents and society. As Pancho Villa is to Alberto, the character of El Pachuco is an alter ego who serves as an audience and reinforcement for Reyna's machismo. El Pachuco is a mythic figure who embodies *pachuco* culture, a youth counterculture tied to zoot suit fashion, specific to East Los Angeles neighborhoods of the 1940s and border culture, as discussed by Durán in "Border Crossings: Images of the Pachuco in Mexican Literature." Seen only by Reyna, El Pachuco moves in and out of the dance club, the family home, the jail cell, and the court room, always immaculately dressed in a zoot suit and quick to wield a switch blade. At every turn, El Pachuco encourages Reyna to fight, seduce, dominate, and remain cynical of institutions. Just as Pancho Villa does with Alberto, El Pachuco frames his advice as tactics for self-defense. The bravado, theatricality, and showy dress of both El Pachuco, wearing a zoot suit, and Pancho Villa, his military garb, root them in Latinx cultural *machismo*. The alter egos suggest that in the absence of a physical audience, these men generate their own audience who remind them of "doing" *machismo* at all times. Alberto and Reyna's true "selves" are in constant tension with a rigid idea of heteronormative, socially constructed masculinity. Both Alberto and Henry feel that they betray Pancho Villa and El Pachuco in rejecting their advice, and both alter egos suffer: Pancho Villa dies again and again, while El Pachuco is assaulted by US sailors during the Zoot Suit Riots. The stakes for preserving or rejecting traditional masculinity is life and death, or at least imagined to be.

In *Straight White Men* we see the social construction and reiteration of masculinity through the three brothers who are each other's audience and reinforcement of socially constructed manhood. After the People in Charge begin the play, Jake and Drew are introduced sitting on the couch, playing video games, and singing songs, before they start wrestling each other. Later, even dancing—and dancing to hip-hop, a genre largely populated by male artists of the global majority—becomes a competition:

> They dance ridiculously, mirroring each other. They do
> a hip-hop dance move, poorly. They do a coordinated
> hoe-down move that culminates in Jake bending Drew

over and humping him from behind. When Drew realizes what's happening, he cheerfully bobs his head and dances along. (Lee 49)

Despite previous comments that assert a reliance on heterosexuality, here masculinity is complicated by allusions to and acceptance of homosexual sex within the freedom of the dance. Later, when all four men dance at the end of Act II, they are at their happiest, most vulnerable, most comfortable, and most free of the expectations and performances of heteronormative masculinity. We see the family as they could be if they stopped performing for each other and society.

Like Alberto, the brothers are self-aware of their privilege—for them as straight, white men. Their parents—particularly their mother, who seems to haunt their interactions but is not a physical character in the play—raised them to be aware of the benefits afforded straight white men; yet all three are unhappy in their lives. Despite their privileges, the aggressive individuality encouraged by socialized gender roles and toxic masculinity remove men from the support of their family and community, rendering them less powerful, more uncertain. Through these visible contradictions, Lee reveals the false promise and fallibility of masculinity as a rigid social construct.

"DOING" MASCULINITIES: USEFULNESS AND ACHIEVEMENT

The men at the center of *Between Pancho Villa and a Naked Woman* and *Straight White Men* share a central paradox: With all the privileges afforded them, what have they accomplished? Or, as Matt would put it, what do they do that is "useful" to anyone other than themselves? (Lee 66). They have spent their lives convincing themselves that they are important because what they do is important. It dawns on them that their pursuits are ultimately self-serving, raising the question of the true power of masculinity. As Matt says, "I spent my whole life trying to make things better, and everything I did just made things worse!" (72).

Masculinities as constructed and performed within the patriarchy are designed for the individual to dominate all others, but that individuality runs counter to other tenets. Particularly in the West and under capitalism, a man's worth and status are linked to his work and career. Men must provide for their families, and within that structure, there is an unspoken hierarchy of work that is more and less associated with masculinity. Jake and Ed believe that the way to help Matt is to help him practice for a job interview, for instance, but Matt is no longer willing or able to inflate his achievements: "Um, well at least in my case, I was teaching a bunch of people something I didn't know how to do, that they didn't want to learn" (65). Rather than prioritizing community and the common good, a patriarchal system of heteronormative masculinity thrives in a hierarchical environment that pits individuals against each other. That is the insurmountable tension at the heart of their conflict. To be useful to others is to elevate others and to put their needs before your own. Matt interprets this as getting out of the way, choosing to be helpful to and caring for his father. However, caregiving is often a role for women, and by the end of the play, Ed is no longer willing to accept his eldest son "cooking and cleaning like a housemaid" (71). This statement again reinforces traditional manhood and masculinity as the opposites of womanhood and femininity.

CONCLUSION: SATIRE AND SYMPATHY

Straight White Men and *Between Pancho Villa and a Naked Woman* are funny plays, drawing on satire, farce, and humor related to heightened performances of gender, manhood, and masculinities. But they are also tragedies. In a tragic dramatic premise, the protagonist does not address their fatal flaw at all, in time, or enough to attain what they need, and this leads to their destruction, loss, or suffering. Unable to reconcile the paradox of a masculinity that promotes the self and self-serving behaviors and their hypothetical desire to serve the common good, the men in these plays fail to change. We watch tragedies to learn what *not* to do when facing similar conflicts. So what are the alternatives?

Berman and Lee write their men satirically but also sympathetically. Their characters seem trapped in and bewildered by patriarchy, and even if they claim to want to resist it, it is so pervasive that these men ultimately feel powerless to do so. Change seems futile. Yet the playwrights are careful to present options, choices, and alternatives to make it clear to their audiences that these men *can* change their behavior. Change requires them to evolve their understanding of masculinity. Patriarchy gives these men the luxury of time, space, and resources to work through their existential crises over years and lifetimes, even across generations.

Invoking the audience, *Straight White Men*'s Person in Charge 2 offers, "As foreign as they are to us, we're gonna try to find some understanding for straight white men. That's what we wish everyone would do for us" (Lee 11). While these characters do not even attempt to understand a more expansive view of gender, masculinity, or sexuality and instead strive to dominate others, bending them to their will and worldviews, the audience quickly realizes that approach is not useful to anyone but the men. Though Lee and Berman's plays satirize performative masculinities, they also have sympathy for the men who are trapped by them. Their actions and behaviors have an outsized impact on all others, for good and for naught. Their privileged positions have potential for doing good, but that is only achieved through examination of how conventional masculinities distort the relationship between the self and others. Known for writing from and across historically marginalized identities, Lee and Berman's plays are milestones in staging gender for the way they "other" men and masculinities within patriarchy, making them subjects for observation, reflection, and critique. By conceding to men the centered and privileged places they have historically had in US and Mexican theatre, Lee and Berman offer them opportunities to see themselves and their behaviors through other lenses. What will men see?

FURTHER RESOURCES

Hall, Katori. *The Mountaintop*. Dramatists Play Service, 2011.
In this play, Katori Hall considers gender and the white male patriarchy on multiple levels, most particularly in the way she complicates Dr. Martin Luther King, Jr., who, on the eve of his assassination, reflects on his legacy as a Civil Rights icon and Great Person of History, but also as a flawed man.

Parks, Suzan Lori. *Topdog/Underdog*. Dramatists Play Service, 2001.
Two brothers, Lincoln and Booth, clash over how to best get ahead in a world that is unkind to Black men.

Reza, Yasmina. *Art*. Translated by Christopher Hampton. Dramatists Play Service, 2007.
An examination of masculinity and friendship, three men turn a disagreement about a painting into criticisms of each other and an examination of their longstanding friendship.

Valdez, Luis. *Zoot Suit and Other Plays*. Arte Público Press, 1992.
This collection of three plays by Valdez includes *Zoot Suit* and offers an examination of machismo and Chicano masculinities as well as immigration as it relates to gender.

REFERENCES

Berman, Sabina. Shelley Tepperman, translator. *Between Pancho Villa and a Naked Woman / Entre Pancho Villa y Una Mujer Desnuda*. NoPassport Press, 1997.

Bien, Abby. "All the Female Playwrights Who Have Had Plays on Broadway." New York Theatre Guide. October 3, 2023. https://www.newyorktheatreguide.com/theatre-news/news/all-the-female-playwrights-who-have-had-plays-on-broadway. Accessed October 10, 2023.

Butler, Judith. *Gender Trouble: Feminism and the Subversion of Identity*. Routledge, 2006.

Ceballos, Miriam. "Machismo: A Culturally Constructed Concept." Master's thesis, California State University, Fresno, CA, 2013. ScholarWorks. https://scholarworks.calstate.edu/concern/theses/vx021g65w. Accessed January 15, 2024.

Durán, Javier. "Border Crossings: Images of the Pachuco in Mexican Literature." *Studies in 20th and 21st Century Literature*, vol. 25, no. 1, 2001.

Lee, Young Jean. *Straight White Men*. Dramatists Play Service, 2017.

Mendoza, Eunice. "Machismo Literature Review." Center for Public Safety Initiatives, 2012.

Whitehead, Stephen and Frank Barrett, eds. *The Masculinities Reader*. Polity, 2002.

Chapter 10

Refuting Narratives of Newness, Constructing Transgender Community

Nicolas Shannon Savard

In the past five years, Broadway has welcomed a handful of **transgender** and nonbinary actors to the commercial theatre stage. In January of 2018, Peppermint of *RuPaul's Drag Race* fame became the first out trans woman to originate a role in a Broadway musical in *Head over Heels*. That summer, Kate Bornstein and Ty Defoe made their Broadway debuts in Young Jean Lee's *Straight White Men*. Notably, with this play, Lee also was the first Asian American woman playwright to have her work produced on Broadway. By 2022, L. Morgan Lee (*A Strange Loop*) became the first out trans actor to be nominated for a Tony Award. In 2023, Alex Newell and J. Harrison Ghee were the first out nonbinary actors to win Tony Awards for their roles in *Shucked* and *Some Like it Hot*, respectively. While Newell and Ghee's awards are a testament to their talent and hard work, it is not a coincidence that the first year nonbinary actors won the award was the same year that the Tonys eliminated the traditional gendered categories of Best Actor and Best Actress. It begs the question: How many other theatre artists' work has gone unrecognized because their identities, bodies, cultural backgrounds—the stories that make up their lives—did not fit neatly within the categories available in the commercial theatre?

Notably, it is also only in the past five years that a Broadway production has hired its first all-women design team with *Lifespan of a Fact* in 2018 (Fierberg) and staged work by an Indigenous American playwright with Larissa Fasthorse's *Thanksgiving Play* in 2023. These milestones are often held

DOI: 10.4324/9781003272854-11

up as indications of the progress of marginalized communities, but they also point to a long history of exclusion. When we uncritically celebrate the first person from a marginalized group to break another of the theatre industry's glass ceilings, it makes it all too easy to assume that our stories, art, and community are new. These stories and artists have long been creating and working in the field. That in mind, this chapter aims to contextualize contemporary US transgender performing artists' work within longer and larger traditions of queer, feminist, and woman of color activism and aesthetics, rather than focusing on individual milestone achievements. In doing so, I aim to illuminate how trans performance builds upon practices of enacting community and cultural-political critique.

Two case studies serve as strong entry points for exploring the themes above: Scott Turner Schofield's *Becoming a Man in 127 EASY Steps* and Dane Figueroa Edidi's *For Black Trans Girls Who Gotta Cuss a Motherf***** Out When Snatching an Edge Ain't Enough*. Press coverage of both Schofield and Edidi often emphasizes their position as the "first" trans artist to break into their respective industries. In 2015, Schofield became the first out trans actor to play a recurring role on American daytime TV (*The Bold and the Beautiful*) and, in 2020, the first out trans man to receive an Emmy nomination (*Studio City*). In 2019, Edidi became the first out trans woman and trans person of color playwright to receive a professional production in Washington, DC with her solo adaptation of the Greek tragedy, *Klytemnstra,* for which she won the Helen Hayes Award in playwriting (Savard, *Queer Legacies*). Both actively resist that narrative of being the "first," instead rooting themselves in longstanding aesthetic traditions and challenging audiences to critically examine the cultural and political forces that contribute to trans, queer, and BIPOC artists' marginalization.

SCOTT TURNER SCHOFIELD

Before Scott Turner Schofield landed his history-making role on daytime television, he spent 15 years touring across the United States and Europe with his autobiographical solo shows. When I asked him about how he chose that path in a 2022 interview on *Gender Euphoria, the Podcast*, he said, simply, "I got into this because there was no other way" (Savard, "On Being a Trans Trailblazer"). In 2000, although he was excelling in his courses in his acting program at Emory University, when it came to the school's mainstage and local professional productions he explained, "I just couldn't get cast in any of them because my gender expression was different. I wasn't an ingenue. I wasn't feminine enough. I wasn't masculine enough" (Savard, "On Being a Trans Trailblazer"). In other words, all the roles available at the time were both written and cast with cisgender actors in mind.

Cisgender describes characters and actors whose gender identity (internal sense of self) and gender expression (self-styled with hair, clothing, vocal quality, gesture, etc.) are aligned with both their sex assigned at birth (male or female) and **gender attribution** (the way others perceive them). "Cis" is a prefix meaning on the same side; it is often used in contrast to "trans," a prefix meaning across, between, or beyond. The experience that Schofield describes from his early theatrical career is distinctly transgender. His gender expression fell somewhere beyond or between the traditional masculinity and femininity of the characters as written. Directors could not instantaneously identify and categorize him as a woman or a man. Autobiographical solo performance offered a way for Schofield to write himself onto the stage, as it has for many transgender actors whose gender expression does not align with directors' expectations.

Because its meaning has shifted since Schofield's early shows, it is important to contextualize what the word "transgender" has meant historically. Today, dominant pop cultural representations of transgender people are fairly narrow. Generally speaking, "transgender" is used to describe individuals who are "born in the wrong body" and seek medical intervention to align our bodies with our gender identities. While this does reflect some trans folks' experience, the popular description is incomplete. Trans historian Susan Stryker traces the emergence of the term "transgender" in the US to the early 1990s. She points to Holly Boswell's 1991 essay "The Transgender

Alternative," as the first to introduce this language on a relatively large scale through the nationally circulated community magazine, *Chrysalis Quarterly*. Boswell proposed "transgender" as a term encompassing all people whose gender identity or expression fell outside of social norms for men and women. By 1992, it gained traction in activist organizing spaces through Leslie Feinberg's pamphlet, *Transgender Liberation*. Later that year, Sandy Stone brought it into academic discussions in the newly developing fields of queer and feminist theory with her essay "The Empire Strikes Back: A Posttranssexual Manifesto" (Stryker 153–158). Rather than describing an individual, internal experience, "transgender" was explicitly rooted in community and was intended to build social and political coalition among a diverse group of people with a wide variety of gender identities and expressions.

Although not yet welcomed into the commercial theatre industry, in the 1980s and 1990s, transgender creatives were in active conversation and community with queer, feminist, and other activist performance collectives. During this time, autobiographical solo performance and performance poetry proliferated as a mode of identity exploration, political consciousness raising, cultural critique, and self-authorship. Queer solo performance particularly flourished in spaces like New York's PS 122 and the lesbian feminist "home for wayward girls" the WOW Café (Hughes and Román 13). Artists who were marginalized in other theatrical venues found community among others who sought to complicate and expand notions of race, class, gender, and sexuality on stage.

Scott Turner Schofield connected with this community by way of Holly Hughes and David Román's 1998 anthology of queer solo performance, *O Solo Homo*. He recounted his initial response upon reading the text:

> There was a whole iceberg of queer theater out there, while I stood on the mainstream theater boat praying for a crash. Wild in the eyes and heart, I approached my queer literature professor, Julie Abraham [...] 'This is the kind of theater I want to make!' I shouted. (Schofield 11)

It led him to a role as a research assistant in the summer of 2000, documenting the history of the WOW Café under the direction of solo artists Holly Hughes and Alina Troyano (a.k.a. Carmelita Tropicana). Schofield cites this experience as particularly formative in shaping his artistic sensibility, developing an understanding of his trans identity, and inspiring his first solo show, *Underground Transit* (Savard, "On Being a Trans Trailblazer").

Across his three solo shows: *Underground Transit, Debutante Balls,* and *Becoming a Man in 127 EASY Steps,* Schofield blends conversational yet vivid storytelling and poetry and completely disintegrates the "fourth wall" dividing actor and audience. The nonlinear, parallel, intersecting, and contrasting narrative structures in his work, linking the personal and the political are also key features of the work of his mentors: Holly Hughes, Carmelita Tropicana, Tim Miller. Also reminiscent of both Carmelita Tropicana and Tim Miller's work is the intimate relationship that Schofield establishes with his audience. Rather than passive spectators, audience members are cast as witnesses to Schofield's experience and to one another; they are asked to be active participants and co-creators of the performance. The playfulness of his gender presentation paired with wry observation and critique resonate with the work of Peggy Shaw (*Menopausal Gentleman,* Split Britches) and Kate Bornstein (*Gender Outlaw, Hidden: A Gender*).

His performances equally draw upon queer and feminist theory, often connecting and translating those academic discourses to his own and the audience's embodied experience. As he explains:

> Onstage with just a backpack full of costumes, I began performing the ways in which a body can—and will—box itself and burst out of that box again and again. Judging by the audience response, those queer theorists were right: Gender is a performance. The magic of live theatre made emotional sense out of the intellectual theory. (Schofield 113)

Schofield's longest-running and most recent show, *Becoming a Man in 127 EASY Steps,* offers a clear example of how he builds upon the work of his queer-feminist theory and performance predecessors and bursts out of the boxes of theatrical conventions.

BECOMING A MAN IN 127 EASY STEPS

Becoming a Man in 127 EASY Steps is Schofield's most ambitious show, reflecting his ever-evolving understanding of gender. When he began touring the show in 2007, there were only 16 stories. The live performance has since morphed into a transmedia storytelling project comprising 127 stories presented in film shorts, a podcast series, and a poetry and prose memoir.[1] Since it is (intentionally) impossible to fit all the stories into a single performance—the touring show averaged between six and eight of the stories per night—the audience is tasked with choosing which ones they will hear (Savard, "On Being a Trans Trailblazer"). In doing so, they take on an active and conscious role in the shaping the meaning of the show. In *Becoming a Man in 127 EASY Steps*, spectators literally help construct the world in which the performance will take place by building a blanket fort which envelops the stage. The stage directions following the opening monologue read, "TURNER enlists the audience to help assemble the fort correctly, pulling panels of white fabric to the back of the seating risers and attaching them with clothespins to the clotheslines" (Schofield 76). Turner then distributes props from a toy box which audience members must hold until he is ready to tell the story which corresponds with each object. Setting the scene inside of a collectively built fort in which Turner shares his "toys" with the audience invokes a sense of play with the spectators. Much like in child's play, the audience is invited to imagine infinite possibilities for the story they will hear.

The first toy that Turner takes up to establish this theme of expansiveness in storytelling is the decoder ring:

> The decoder ring which is also printed on programs, appears on the screen. It looks like pie chart slices individually marked by such labels as "Gay," "Male," "Passing," "Heterosexual,"' etc. These words correspond

Fig. 10.1 Turner in the fort. *Becoming a Man in 127 EASY Steps*, directed by Steve Bailey, Capitol Hill Arts Center (Seattle, WA). Photo by Alain Fonterey.

to numbers, running 0 through 9 around the edge of the ring. (82–83)

He suggests that this device could be used in daily life to approach gender nonconforming people, such as himself, with curiosity. For example:

If you see a person wearing a dress who's seven feet tall with an Adam's apple, you know there's a story there. How much nicer would it be for someone to take those visual cues, align them against a nonjudgmental scale, and say, "Hey, give me story number 53," rather than "What the fuck are you, freak?" (83)

The metaphor serves to address the ways in which gender non-conforming people are often met with ridicule and the pressure that is put on us to explain our gender presentation and identities as the price of existing in public. He demonstrates the way the game will work, asking the audience to "call out a number according to what you see in me" (83). Giving the example of number 127, he explains:

> Why 127? Well, it's prime and kind of a complicated mouthful, like me, and it's part of my social security number, which says EVERYTHING about my identity, apparently. Oh, I'm just begging for someone to steal MY identity, you could get... *(The numbers 1, 2, and 7 correspond to stealth, queer, and body.)* Your very own stealth queer body! Or any number of other things. So now it's your turn. What do you see? What story would you like to hear? They almost never match up, what you see and what you get, but we'll have a good time getting there. (83; italics in original)

While the audience of one performance may hear the stories they ask for, there are always more combinations of Turner's identities, always more possibilities of stories to be told. The narrative that ends up being heard is the one that the audience reads onto him. Simultaneously, they are made aware of incomplete nature of the narrative; in other words, the sum of all the stories they hear in one performance will not "add up" to a singular, coherent plot and resolution (Savard, *Queer Legacies*).

Using the decoder ring as a metaphor, Schofield makes the concept of gender performativity concrete and uses it to frame the audience's role in shaping the story. Introduced by Judith Butler in her book, *Gender Trouble: Feminism and the Subversion of Identity* (1990), gender performativity is the process of how gender is socially constructed. Butler argues that gender is a performance, but it is not fake or costume that one can take on and off. Rather, the performances Butler references are day-to-day, moment-by-moment acts: our choices in clothing, hair style, mannerisms, vocal patterns, movements, and modes of interacting with others. Together, these daily performances create our gender expression, which we use to communicate our identities to other people. We are all performing gender, consciously or not, all the time. Much like Schofield articulates in his explanation of the decoder ring, the social construction of gender depends as much on how it is performed (gender expression) as it does on how the audience interprets it (gender attribution).

Throughout the show, Turner invites the audience to co-construct his gendered performance. At times the interdependent nature of that performance is deeply intimate. In "Story Section 1, 3: Get a Tattoo," Turner brings an audience member onto the stage; if they have a tattoo and want to "show and tell," he invites them to. Then, the stage directions

Fig. 10.2 Turner takes his testosterone shot. Photo by Alain Fonterey.

indicate, "TURNER affixes each of them with one-half of a fake tattoo. The tattoo is a replica of Picasso's *Matador*. The audience member chooses whether to be the matador or the bull" (86). As he does so, he delivers a poem: "I want you to accept my skin/ I've been tattooing memories there, / and my body is a quilt I would wrap you in/ as though you were a guest in my home" (86). The direct, physical connection with an individual member of the audience is reminiscent of performances by Schofield's mentors. For example, in *My Queer Body* Tim Miller sits on an audience member's lap and holds their hand to his bare chest, asking them to feel his heartbeat; in honor of her own performance art mentor, Jack Smith, Carmelita Tropicana chops an onion on stage to produce tears, inviting the audience to inhale and "cry with me" ("Cry a la Jack").

At other times, Turner's interactions with the audience are far more playful. For example, in "Story Section 2, 3: Tie a Tie" Turner must tie a tie as fast as he can while the audience hums the theme song to the popular TV quiz show *Jeopardy!* (96). Tying the tie becomes a performance of masculinity, and the audience is asked to enact a kind of comedic pressure for him to showcase his skill (or lack thereof) in this performance of manhood. By contrast, in the story that immediately follows, the tie makes another appearance and takes on a much higher-stakes meaning. Turner stands before the judge who will decide whether or not to grant his request to legally change his name and gender marker. As the judge looks him over, evaluating the authenticity of his performance of masculinity, Turner narrates his inner monologue: "I hope my tie is straight. Suddenly the appearance of the knot is all that stands between me and that M on my driver's license. If only I had gone for the Windsor knot instead of the four-in-hand" (96–98). What had been a silly and seemingly arbitrary performance of masculinity in the previous scene becomes something that could make or break whether he is seen as a man in the judge's eyes and, by extension, in the eyes of the government.

While Turner's onstage storytelling embodies an interdependent construction of gender, Schofield's writing about the show further emphasizes trans community. His introduction to the

script credits fellow trans artists Kate Bornstein for dramaturgy and S. Bear Bergman for the title, *Becoming a Man
in 127 EASY Steps* (Schofield 73). In his acknowledgments,
he thanks additional members of his "trans artist family"
including Ryka Aoki, T Cooper, Sean Dorsey, Imani Henry,
Angela Motter, and Katz/Athens Boys Choir (120). Even as
a writer-performer of one-person shows, Schofield ensures
that his story is one among a constellation of other trans
narratives.

LADY DANE FIGUEROA EDIDI

Like Scott Turner Schofield, Lady Dane Figueroa Edidi has
been celebrated as the first out trans woman of color to have
her work recognized and produced by professional theaters in
Washington, DC. Her plays, in both their subject matter and
aesthetics, are deeply rooted in Black and Indigenous trans
history, honoring those who have come before her and making space for a multiplicity of Black trans stories. Her play
For Black Trans Girls embodies how Edidi is in conversation
with other Black queer feminist artists and how she combats
the historical and cultural erasure of trans women of color.

Edidi wrote *For Black Trans Girls Who Gotta Cuss a
Motherf***** Out When Snatching an Edge Ain't Enough*
as an homage to Ntozake Shange's, *for colored girls who
have considered suicide/when the rainbow is enuf* (Edidi,
"Interview"). In responding directly to *for colored girls*, she
situates herself within the lineage of both Shange's work and
that of Black women and queer of color theatrical jazz practitioners who have similarly built upon the 1973 choreopoem.[2]

Shange's signature theatrical intervention, the choreopoem,
blends performance poetry and African American jazz traditions. The compilation of poems, performed as solos and
ensemble pieces, is closer to poetry set to movement and
music than a traditional play. Breaking from Aristotelian
uses of poetry to construct plot, philosophical argument,
and *universal* protagonists,[3] Shange's choreopoem employs
poetry to explore the *specificity* of Black women's embodied

experiences and perspectives. Rather than a single protagonist, a linear plot, or chronological time, the piece is structured relationally with the women each telling stories in the first person as a means of connecting with one another. Like the jazz music from which it draws inspiration, it is fundamentally an ensemble-based form. The choreopoem highlights voices while maintaining an emphasis on how those voices harmonize and complement the whole.[4]

Stylistically, *For Black Trans Girls* is written in similar lyrical, rhythmic poetry. It is performed by an ensemble of four Black trans women who at times represent specific characters, yet their roles are not fixed. The experiences Edidi writes for the stage are highly specific as well as deeply connected to and critical of systemic injustices. Much like *for colored girls*, this choreopoem speaks to Edidi's own experience and shared experiences among Black women, and specifically Black trans women (Edidi, "Interview"). *For Black Trans Girls* weaves together rich imagery, snapshots of moments in individual Black trans women's lives, and incisive critique of colonial, white supremacist, and patriarchal histories and contemporary structures.

Edidi borrows the structure of *for colored girls*, opening with a ritual and proclamation of who the piece is written for. The prologue defines the breadth of experiences of trans womanhood to which it speaks:

> This book for Black Trans Girls
> Black Trans Women
> Gender non conforming
> Non Binary
> Ghetto
> Boujie
> Bruja
> Banjee
> Bitch
> Queen
> Goddess
> Heaux
> Priestess

> Two Spirit
> Red Marsh
> Trans
> Woman. (Edidi, *For Black Trans Girls* 12)

She calls out to artists, nerds, traditional nine-to-five working girls, poor girls, sex workers, disabled trans girls, those who have been embraced by their families and those who had to find their own, the living and the dead. As the prologue ends, she makes direct reference to Shange's choreopoem, declaring

> This Book For
> Black Trans Girls Who Considered suicide when the
> Rainbow ain't never been enough
> This Book for
> Black Trans Girls Who Gotta Cuss a Mother Fucker Out
> When Snatching an Edge ain't enough
> Because a bitch tried it
> And wanna know how tough you are
> Because
> YOU WISH A MOTHER FUCKER WOULD
> Because
> you should have hymns
> and
> psalms
> And
> love poems written in praise of your name
> Sisters
> What a shame this world be basic as shit. (16)

This moment lays out the purpose of the choreopoem: to hold all aspects of a multifaceted Black trans experience of womanhood when the world refuses to acknowledge it. In contrast to the reductive, tragic frame through which trans lives are portrayed in mainstream media, Edidi insists on singing hymns, psalms, and love poems. She insists that Black trans girls are as sacred and deserving of affection as they are tough and capable of "cussing a motherfucker out." These truths coexist. She maintains the sacred, spiritual tone as she moves into the "Invocation/Ritual." Again, she emphasizes a duality of joy and pain as she explains what is to come:

> We gather here prepared to summon the dead
> To birth the living
> And foreshadow what joy there is to be had
> We illuminate mind
> To pain
> To past
> To what elation can be
> When we
> Are loved. (21)

In the next breath, she sets parameters for the role of the audience, specifically those who do not belong to Black and Brown trans communities, stating,

> We are gathered here
> Priestesses
> Goddesses
> Griot
> Greatly
> granting you permission to observe
> But if you believe your role is one of voyeur
> Or that you will bear witness to trauma porn
> You have come to the wrong church. (21)

This "permission to observe" is a direct challenge to how transgender people, and particularly transgender women of color, are typically treated in the media and popular culture and how cisgender audiences consequently view the community. Framing the trans women speaking to the audience as "Priestesses/Goddesses/Griot"[5] places them in a position of power as figures to be revered. It serves to reinforce the message about who the piece is intended to center and celebrate and sets clear boundaries for how straight-cis and white audiences are expected to interact. The religious references embedded in the invocation establish the theater as a sacred space for honoring the stories shared, adding a sense of gravity to what the audience is about to witness. At the same time, it forecloses the possibility of reading these trans stories through the objectifying lens the mainstream media uses to titillate viewers (Savard, *Queer Legacies*).

Many of the pieces we bear witness to throughout the choreopoem are rooted in loving relationships, moments between individuals; they expand outward to cultural and structural critique at the level of nations. The political is never divorced from the personal; rather, systems of oppression come into sharp focus within the speaker's telling of her story. For example, the solo "Man of War" begins: "When Hugh and I first met, / He was sexy as fuck" (Edidi, *For Black Trans Girls* 71). She recounts the scene of their initial flirtation in the bookstore where she worked, falling in love, getting married in a dress with a train that "extended the length to eternity and back baby" (73). After painting the picture of their romance, she turns to the argument they had and her protest the day the army called Hugh back into service. The scene foreshadows the following stanza:

> When the call came
> Said Hugh won't be returning
> Said he died defending his country
> This country
> A country that doesn't even find it important to call him
>   he
> A country that now tells me we ain't really married
> A country that tells me I ain't really She
> A country that props up a racist bully
> and call him president
> He left me for a country
> That to me ain't never been kind
> Left me to a country
> That constantly mistreats me and mine
> Even when we die for them. (75)

The story is one of profound loss, but it refuses a simple tragic framing. She may be a grieving wife of a fallen soldier; at the same time, she brings forth multiple layers of tension between the cultural and political forces responsible for her loss, making her a widow, and the same state not recognizing her in that role. Echoing earlier pieces which explicitly eschew narratives of "trauma porn" and the "damsel in distress," this broad view reflects an overarching goal of Edidi's writing. She describes her characters as Black trans women seeking accountability, sometimes taking matters into their own hands to get it (Edidi, "Interview"). Edidi's political critique lies in where the speaker's grief, anger, and sense of betrayal are directed. The speaker does not mention a specific person or event that killed Hugh; rather, she attacks interlocking systems: the legal system that won't recognize his identity or their marriage, the tens of millions of people who voted Donald Trump into the White House in 2016, the country that systemically endorses white supremacy. Edidi published *For Black Trans Girls* in 2017, in the wake of the 2016 US presidential election and the beginning of the current wave of anti-trans legislation across the country. While "Man of War" responds directly to contemporary national politics, the choreopoem exposes the overlaps between state-sanctioned transphobia and white supremacy throughout the nation's history.

Blending the personal and political, the next poem begins with a demand from an "old white cis man" to know, "What does your generation know of the AIDS crisis?" In reply, the speaker introduces Aunt Jimmy: "I/ loved my Trans Aunt/ She spoiled me with anything my little Trans Black girl/ heart desired" (82). In claiming her trans aunt's story as a narrative of the AIDS crisis, she writes her family, and specifically Black trans women, into a history that has primarily focused on the experiences of white cisgender men. She further resists trans erasure from this history, explaining, "My Aunt Jimmy wasn't afforded gender freedom/ Relegated to only celebrating her womanhood/ by way of her drag persona." Her womanhood is affirmed in descriptions of her in performance as "the Belle of the Ball" and "glamorous" as well as the claim, "They say her dance beguiled men of their wits/ and/ their wallets" (82). The celebratory image is later contrasted with a community washed over with "hysteria/ rage/ abandonment/ despair," which characterized the AIDS crisis of the 1980s. Much like in "Man of War," the speaker directs her own rage toward the President; in this case, holding both President Reagan himself and the state at large accountable for their inaction, saying,

Old ass
Racist ass
Classist ass

> Pretend War on Drugs because he don't give a fuck
> about the American people ass
> Reagan
> Gleefully
> ignored the pleas of the people to find a cure
> or
> at least
> cultivate funds towards effective research. (85)

Focusing on the personal impacts of national politics, the poem shifts to much more intimate images: gay, trans, and drag queen friends "whose laughter dressed our homes in glee/began to disappear" and "tears left on the floors of our homes" (85–86). Turning back to the white gay man who'd posed the initial question, the speaker ends the piece with, "You/ lost your friends/ I/ lost my mothers" (87). While the poem is a depiction of profound loss and grief, so too is it a reclamation of narratives erased. That purpose is most clearly embodied in the lines, "Search/ through history/ for those who ain't make it/ Made it" (85). Insisting upon Aunt Jimmy's inclusion in the story of the AIDS crisis at once holds space for individual grief and claims space for Black trans women in a too-often whitewashed history. Ultimately, the poem's images of celebratory, joyous, intergenerational, and intersectional queer-trans community alongside the impacts of the virus on individual bodies and families paints a more complex picture of the 1980s than our cultural narratives usually offer.

WHY DO WE BELIEVE TRANS THEATRE IS NEW?

While the mainstream theatre industry frames transgender stories and artists as "new," the reasons for that perception run deeper than individual biases or exclusion from Broadway stages. The erasure of trans lives at the structural and cultural level, compounded by intersectional oppressions, makes locating trans histories by traditional methods challenging. As both Scott Turner Schofield and Lady Dane Figueroa Edidi point to in their work, the United States, culturally and politically, has an ongoing legacy of invalidating, neglecting, criminalizing, and enacting violence upon gender nonconforming people. Official records often do not reflect how transgender people show up in our day-to-day lives; whether due to inaccessibility, legalized discrimination, or safety concerns, personal histories tend to be fragmented in their documentation. Beyond the stories that go undocumented, far more have been suppressed through colonial violence. Part of the project of European colonization in the Americas and across the globe was imposing rigid gender norms, forcing many Indigenous peoples with more expansive cultural understandings of gender to assimilate into white Catholic and Protestant ideals of masculinity and femininity.[6]

While legal records of trans lives tend to misrepresent our stories, the cultural documentation of trans performance, when it is present at all, is inconsistent. The evidence from which theatre historians can piece together the details of a production, an actor's career, or a play's cultural impact typically consists of the ephemera kept in archives and reviews published in newspapers. Where do we look for evidence when the theaters producing trans artists' work do not have an archive? Or when our primary performance venues are not theatre spaces at all? Where do we look for evidence for the plays that never received reviews because of where they were presented and who was on stage? What happens when the only review was written by a reporter who missed most of the nuance of the story because he had no context for trans experiences? How many of the "male impersonators" touring the vaudeville circuit lived as men off stage? The language with which trans art and stories have been recorded historically, and to a large extent today, rarely reflects the ways in which we describe ourselves.

Both Scott Turner Schofield and Lady Dane Figueroa Edidi were drawn to autobiographical performance and the choreopoem because of the ways those forms allowed them to write themselves onto the stage. The way that they each emphasize community in their work makes their performances in and of themselves additionally valuable for the study of transgender theatre history. Through their scripts, we can access their perspectives directly rather than filtered through the lens of a reviewer. Although traditionally theatre history tends to focus on individual stars, it may be more useful to look for evidence of community when searching for trans theatre histories. Who have trans artists been in conversation with? Whose footsteps are we following in? Whose stories do we write back into the historical record by writing them onto the stage? Both Schofield and Edidi's performance work and writing provide evidence that they are not the "first," that transgender stories are not new. Their accomplishments as individual artists and the milestones their work represent for trans visibility in the theatre are absolutely worthy of celebration. Equally worthy of recognition and celebration are the ways that they actively bring queer, transgender, Black, and women's histories onto the stage with them.

FURTHER RESOURCES

Gossett, Reina, et al., eds. *Trap Door: Trans Cultural Production and the Politics of Visibility*. MIT Press, 2017.
A collection of printed images, interviews, and critical essays from 36 contributors covering trans art, performance, activism, and cultural history from the 1960s to today.
Keyes, Leanna, et al., eds. *The Methuen Drama Book of Trans Plays*. Methuen Drama/Bloomsbury Publishing, 2021.
The first-of-its-kind anthology of eight plays by trans and nonbinary authors, each accompanied by a critical scholarly essay.
Stryker, Susan. *Transgender History: The Roots of Today's Revolution*. 2nd edn., Seal Press, 2017.
An overview of the development of transgender activism, identity, language, and community in the United States from the 1850s to 2017.

REFERENCES

Bornstein, Kate. *Gender Outlaw: On Men, Women, and the Rest of Us*. 2nd edn., Vintage Books, 2016.
Boswell, Holly. "The Transgender Alternative." *Chrysalis Quarterly*, vol. 1, no. 2, 1991, pp. 29–31.
Butler, Judith. *Gender Trouble: Feminism and the Subversion of Identity*. Routledge, 1990.
Driskill, Qwo-Li. "Stolen from Our Bodies: First Nations Two-Spirits/Queers and the Journey to a Sovereign Erotic." *Studies in American Indian Literatures*, vol. 16, no. 2, 2004, pp. 50–64.

Edidi, Dane Figueroa. *For Black Trans Girls Who Gotta Cuss a Motherf***** Out When Snatching an Edge Ain't Enough: A Choreo Poem*. Dane Edidi, 2017.

———. "Interview." Conducted by Nicolas Shannon Savard, May 26, 2020.

Feinberg, Leslie. *Transgender Liberation: A Movement Whose Time Has Come*. World View Forum, 1992.

Fierberg, Ruthie. "19 Milestone Broadway Shows of the Decade." *Playbill*, December 31, 2019. https://playbill.com/article/19-milestone-broadway-shows-of-the-decade. Accessed October 6, 2023.

Hughes, Holly, and David Román, eds. *O Solo Homo: The New Queer Performance*. Grove Press, 1998.

Jones, Omi Osun Joni L. *Theatrical Jazz: Performance, Àṣẹ, and the Power of the Present Moment*. Ohio State University Press, 2015.

Miller, Tim. "My Queer Body (1992)." *The Hemispheric Institute Digital Video Library*, 1992. https://hemisphericinstitute.org/en/hidvl-collections/item/2636-tim-miller-body.html. Accessed October 6, 2023.

Savard, Nicolas Shannon, host. "On Being a Trans Trailblazer with Guest Scott Turner Schofield." *Gender Euphoria, the Podcast*, season 1, ep. 9. HowlRound Theatre Commons, March 30, 2022.

———. *Queer Legacies: Tracing the Roots of Contemporary Transgender Performance*. Ohio State University Press, 2021. https://etd.ohiolink.edu/acprod/odb_etd/etd/r/1501/10?clear=10&p10_accession_num=osu1626384633865101. Accessed August 22, 2023.

Schofield, Scott Turner. *Two Truths and a Lie: A Memoir*. Homofactus Press, 2008.

Shange, Ntozake. *for colored girls who have considered suicide, when the rainbow is enuf: a choreopoem*. Scribner Poetry, 1997.

Stone, Sandy. "The Empire Strikes Back: A Posttranssexual Manifesto." *Camera Obscura*, vol. 10, no. 2, 1992, pp. 150–176.

Stryker, Susan. *Transgender History: The Roots of Today's Revolution*. 2nd edn., Seal Press, 2017.

Tropicana, Carmelita. "Cry a la Jack." *The Hemispheric Institute Digital Video Library*, 2005. https://hemisphericinstitute.org/en/hidvl-collections/item/2553-carmelita-jack.html. Accessed October 6, 2023.

NOTES

1 The multimedia version of *Becoming a Man in 127 Easy Steps* can be found at https://www.127steps.com.
2 A few of those artists include Laurie Carlos, Daniel Alexander Jones, Sharon Bridgforth, Djola Branner of Pomo Afro Homos, Shay Youngblood, Robbie McCauley, and D'Lo.

3 "Universal" within the theatre is a term most readily offered to cisgender, heterosexual, white men. Women, BIPOC, queer, and disabled people's stories are frequently cast as "culturally specific" or "fringe" or "special interest" by mainstream audiences, critics, and producers.

4 For further discussion of Shange's work and the jazz aesthetic, see Omi Osun Joni L. Jones's *Theatrical Jazz*.

5 In West African tradition, griot is a storyteller, musician, and orator who passes on the history and oral traditions of their culture and community.

6 "Two Spirit" is an umbrella term proposed by Indigenous scholars, historians, and activists to describe various gender identities beyond man and woman that have and continue to exist within Native cultures. Although similar to the original "transgender," which links a variety of possible gender identities and expressions, the terms are not interchangeable. Two Spirit reflects particular spiritual roles and cultural sovereignty of Indigenous peoples of the Americas. See Driskill.

Glossary

American Indian Movement (AIM) Founded in Minneapolis, MN, in 1968, this grassroots activist group by and for Indigenous people addressed systemic issues of poverty, discrimination, and police brutality against Indigenous people as well as publicly advocated for treaty rights and preservation of culture.

Arab Spring A series of anti-government protests that took place across much of the Arab world in late 2010, continuing for several years.

Black Feminism A feminist theory and approach that centers the experiences of Black women, specifically recognizing their unique position in relation to racism, sexism, and classism, as well as other social and political identities.

Butch/femme Connected to Judith Butler's performativity, this refers to a performative dynamic within lesbian relationships where a "butch" woman presents a more masculine style while her "femme" counterpart presents a more traditionally feminine style.

Capitalist economy An economic system based on a free market to establish the most efficient allocation of resources and price determination based on supply and demand, and a private organization owns the means of production, or "capital."

Choreopoem Attributed to Ntozake Shange's *for colored girls ...*, the choreopoem uniquely combines movement, poetry, and performance.

Cisgender A person whose gender identity is aligned with the sex they were assigned at birth.

Dan A character role-type in Chinese opera, *dan* are female characters. While men and women play *dan* roles, men have most commonly played them since a royal decree banned women from the stage from 1772 to 1923.

Environmental theatre A form of theatre championed by Richard Schechner and The Performing Garage that shifted audience perspectives by using nontraditional theatre spaces that were meant to remain visible during productions. The physical locations—their associations, histories, and material realities—are integral to the productions happening within them.

Feminism A general term for the advocacy of equal rights and opportunities for women and a movement that addresses gender inequality, highlights women's voices, and challenges patriarchal norms while promoting feminist ideals, empowerment, and social change.

First Nations A term commonly used to describe Indigenous peoples of Canada who are ethnically neither Métis nor Inuit.

Gender A term used to describe someone as "male" or "female," "masculine" or "feminine," but based on social constructs and ideas of gender within a particular society, culture, or group.

Gender attribution The process through which others perceive and assign a gender to a person, with or without any knowledge of that person's sex assigned at birth or gender identity.

Gender expression Often classified socially as a binary of "masculine" or "feminine," gender expression is the external manifestation of gender that may be expressed through a person's name, pronouns, clothing, haircut, voice, behavior, etc.

Gender identity A person's innate understanding of their own gender.

Gender performativity Attributed to Judith Butler, gender performativity refers to the ways gender is performed and re-performed in social, cultural, and individual settings, both consciously and unconsciously. It builds on the idea that words bring into effect what they name; in naming ideas of gender, gender roles and "norms," often binaristic, become routinized in societies and cultures. Butler's argument is not that gender is put on, but is a constant negotiation with societal norms and individual. Thus, gender is a complex, repeated, daily performance that is reinforced by society and individuals' conscious and unconscious actions.

Gender stratification The inequalities that exist among genders in regard to wealth, power, and privilege.

Hegemony (or hegemonic) The position of being the strongest, most powerful, and therefore able to control others; referring to the ruling or dominant idea in a social or cultural setting.

Heteronormative/heteronormativity The societal assumption that heterosexuality is the default sexual orientation, often marginalizing and erasing LGBTQ2S identities and relationships and reinforcing traditional gender roles.

Hijab Originally from the word for "curtain" or "partition," this term refers to various head coverings worn by some Muslim women. A hijab can come in many forms, but often specifically refers to a headscarf that leaves the face visible while covering the hair, neck, and ears.

Honor killings Part of "honor crimes," these are connected to a global culture of discrimination and the belief that women are objects and commodities, often under the control of her family (particularly male relatives). Women's bodies hold family honor and some cultures or families conduct "honor killings" of women to preserve familial honor.

Indigenous A broad term frequently used to refer to and honor people who lived on and in relationship with the land well before any settler or colonial context.

INTAR International Arts Relations Theatre was founded by Max Ferrá in 1966 in New York City for Latine playwrights and theatre-makers. Maria Irene Fornés ran its Hispanic Playwrights-in-Residence Laboratory from 1981 to 1992, which provided developmental space for Hispanic playwrights across the US.

Intersectionality   Originated by Kimberlé Crenshaw in 1989, intersectionality is a theory that recognizes the unique ways that systems of oppression impact people's lives according to their identities. Crenshaw specifically wrote about the treatment of Black women in the legal system and the ways that courts overlooked the specific challenges facing them because of their positionality as Black and women. Intersectional is also often used to refer to the multiple identities that inform one's experience in the world.

Machismo   This refers to an idea in Hispanic and Latinx cultures that a man must be "manly" and demonstrate a strong, often exaggerated, sense of masculine pride and power.

Male gaze   A theory created by feminist film scholar Laura Mulvey in 1975 that asserts the cinema and media depict women as objects of desire, catering to the heterosexual male viewer's perspective and reinforcing gender inequality.

Marianismo   A Spanish term that equates with femininity and connects gendered behavior to the Virgin Mary, which emphasizes purity, chaste behavior, and deference to men.

MENA (Middle East and North Africa)   A term used to refer to the specific geographic area. While "Middle East" may be considered problematic in some contexts, it is commonly used because it is more easily translated from English to Arabic and is frequently used internationally. SWANA (South West Asia and North Africa) is another term often used to describe this area.

Metatheatrical   A dramatic technique where a play or performance self-consciously draws attention to its own theatricality, blurring the line between fiction and reality.

Métis   From Latin "to mix," this term often is used in Canada to refer to people of mixed Indigenous and European backgrounds. Legally (a definition established in 2003), Métis refers to descendants of specific historical communities and the people who have and maintain those cultural ties.

Misovire Developed and practiced by Werewere Liking, this refers to the practice of denouncing patriarchal social practices that diminish women, instead re-writing and redefining rituals to foreground the role of women in creative work.

Murdered and Missing Indigenous Women and Girls (MMIWG) The phrase a used to refer to the longstanding human rights crisis of violence against Indigenous women in Canada and the US and the lack of response to Indigenous women's abduction, murder, and disappearance. It also refers to a grassroots movement to raise awareness about the ongoing crisis of missing and murdered Indigenous women and girls and its effects on Indigenous communities.

Narrative prosthesis The term used by Mitchell and Snyder to illustrate the problem with narratives that use disability to signal something is out of place and a character that potentially needs to be saved.

Neo-imperialism A contemporary form of imperialism in which powerful entities use economic, political, cultural, or military means to gain influence and control over other nations or regions. Unlike traditional forms of imperialism, which frequently involve direct colonization and territorial expansion, neo-imperialism operates more subtly via economic and technological dominance to maintain control over others' resources, markets, and geopolitical decisions.

Orientalism A term coined by Edward Said that describes the imitation or depiction of aspects of the Eastern world in a stereotypical way, through the lens of Western, European colonial powers as a way for the West to dominate or gain power.

Patriarchy A social system in which positions of dominance and privilege are primarily held by men.

Postmodern feminism Butler's concept that gender is constructed is one of several crucial ideas that lead feminism away from ideas of gender essentialism (the idea that women are a stable and exclusively biological category) and toward ideas that account for individual perspectives and differences within feminism. This is part of a larger postmodern shift that can also be found in the arts, including theatre.

Settler colonization A system of oppression based on genocide and colonialism that aims to displace people of a nation, typically Indigenous people, in favor of the new settler population and their culture/practices.

Sex assigned at birth Sex assigned to infants at birth, usually based on the superficial appearance of anatomy. "Sex assigned at birth" is more specific than simply "sex," because scholars like Anne Fausto Sterling have pointed to the ways sex is much more complex and cannot be solely determined by anatomy.

Sexuality (sexual orientation) Not to be confused with gender, sexual orientation describes a person's enduring physical, romantic, and/or emotional attraction to another person.

SWANA (South West Asia and North Africa) *See* MENA

Third World feminism Often connected with transnational feminism, Third World feminism looks beyond the white "second-wave" feminist views of 1960s that have historically considered oppression tied to whiteness and gender. Feminists Chanda Talpade Mohanty and Uma Narayan use "Third World" to reclaim and reappropriate the term.

Transgender A term to describe people whose gender identities and/or expressions differ from their sex assigned at birth. Rooted in political and cultural organizing, it is an umbrella term encompassing a wide range of gender identities and expressions that exist between or beyond the strict masculine/male/man vs. feminine/female/woman binary.

Turtle Island Indigenous name for the continent of North America.

Two Spirit An umbrella term proposed by Indigenous scholars, historians, and activists to describe gender identities beyond man and woman that have and continue to exist within Native cultures. While similar to transgender, it is not interchangeable due to the cultural, spiritual connections it holds.

Whiteness A socially and politically constructed behavior and idea that privileges and advantages white people, allowing those socially deemed as white to reap material, economic, political, financial, and structural benefits over others.

White supremacy Systemic racism based on the belief that white people should dominate society because of their presumed racial superiority over others.

Key Moments in Time

As noted in the Introduction, we aim to trouble linear, chronological notions of time, focusing instead on the connections and overlaps to acknowledge our ancestors as well as works and artists who have been erased or ignored in many histories. Consider these moments in time as additional points in our constellation(s).

December 1879 First performance of Henrik Ibsen's *A Doll's House* in Copenhagen, a play that asks powerful questions about gender and gender roles in modern society.

1916 The first known anti-lynching play, *Rachel* by Angelina Weld Grimke, is published.

1919 Mary P. Burrill's *Aftermath* published in *The Liberator*, a socialist magazine.

1921 Zona Gale is the first woman to win Pulitzer Prize in drama for *Miss Lulu Bett*.

1929 Virginia Woolf publishes *A Room of One's Own*.

1934 The Hays Code, a set of guidelines for motion pictures, is imposed. Intended to limit profanity, sex, and violence on screen, it significantly impacts perceptions and portrayals of gender, sexuality, and race in films, and remained in force until 1968.

1959 Lorraine Hansberry's *A Raisin in the Sun* premieres at the Ethel Barrymore Theater (New York), making her the first Black woman produced on a Broadway stage.

1964 Adrienne Kennedy's *Funnyhouse of a Negro* premieres Off-Broadway and wins the Obie Award for Distinguished Play.

1965   Ghanian playwright Ama Ata Aidoo publishes *The Dilemma of a Ghost*, making Aidoo the first published female African dramatist.

1967   Charles Ludlam's Ridiculous Theatrical Company is founded in New York.

June 28, 1969   The Stonewall Uprising, a key moment in queer history and activism. Beginning when the police raid the Stonewall Inn, the demonstrations and protests in response to the anti-queer violence last six days and bring significant visibility to queer rights in the US.

1974   Caryl Churchill is named the Royal Court's (London) first female playwright-in-residence.

1975   Laura Mulvey publishes "Visual Pleasure and Narrative Cinema," introducing the "male gaze."

1976   Spiderwoman Theatre is founded in New York.

Ntozake Shange's *for colored girls* ... opens in New York, becoming the second play by a Black woman on Broadway.

Anna Mae Aquash's body is discovered in South Dakota. No one would be charged for her murder for 27 years.

1977   Combahee River Collective Statement, a key document in contemporary Black Feminism, is published by the Combahee River Collective, a Black Feminist Lesbian organization active 1974–1980.

Maria Irene Fornés's *Fefu and Her Friends* premieres.

1979   Caryl Churchill's *Cloud 9* premieres.

Werewere Liking's *The Power of Um* premieres.

October 1980   WOW, an international women's theatre festival is established, organized by Lois Weaver and Peggy Shaw. Only 18 months later, WOW Café Theatre is created as an experimental performance venue for lesbian-feminist and queer women artists.

1980   Split Britches is founded.

1982   Caryl Churchill's *Top Girls* premieres.

1984 Tess Onwueme's *The Broken Calabash* premieres.

1986 Griselda Gambaro's *Antígona furiosa* is performed in Buenos Aires. (The play is not published until 1989, while Gambaro is in exile in Barcelona.)

1988 *M. Butterfly* premieres on Broadway, starring John Lithgow and BD Wong. (A revival, featuring a significant revision of the script, premiers on Broadway in 2017.)

Tess Onwueme's *The Reign of Wazobia* is performed.

1989 Feminist legal scholar/activist Kimberlé Crenshaw publishes "Demarginalizing the Intersection of Race and Sex: A Black Feminist Critique of Antidiscrimination Doctrine, Feminist Theory and Antiracist Politics," introducing the term "intersectionality."

Mahesh Dattani's *Dance Like a Man* is first performed in Bangalore.

1993 Sabina Berman's *Between Pancho Villa and a Naked Woman* premieres in Mexico (adapted to film in 1996).

1997 Manjula Padmanabhan's *Harvest* wins Onassis Prize for Theatre in Greece.

Paula Vogel's *How I Learned to Drive* premieres Off-Broadway and wins the Pulitzer Prize for Drama in 1998.

1998 First performance of Yvette Nolan's *Annie Mae's Movement* in Whitehorse, Yukon, Canada.

1999 Judith Butler publishes *Gender Trouble*.

2002 The Turtle Gals Performance Ensemble performs *The Scrubbing Project*.

2006 Werewere Liking's *Sogolon* premieres.

Survivor and activist Tarana Burke founds the Me Too Movement, which sees a resurgence via social media (#MeToo) in 2017.

2007 Scott Turner Schofield begins touring first versions of *Becoming a Man in 127 EASY Steps*.

2013 *Shakespeare's Sisters* is developed at Al-Harah Theatre in Beit Jala (Occupied Palestine).

2014 Lois Weaver's *What Tammy Needs to Know about Getting Old and Having Sex* premieres at La Mama.

2016 Hanane Hajj Ali performs *Jogging: Theatre in Progress* throughout Lebanon, touring globally through 2019.

Lady Dane Figueroa Edidi publishes *For Black Trans Girls …*

2017 Paula Vogel's *Indecent* premieres on Broadway.

2018 Adrienne Kennedy's *He Brought Her Heart Back in a Box* premieres; Kennedy is inducted to the Theater Hall of Fame.

Young Jean Lee becomes first Asian American produced on Broadway with *Straight White Men.*

Heather Raffo's *Noura* is performed.

Peppermint is the first out trans woman to originate a role in a Broadway musical (*Head over Heels*).

2022 L. Morgan Lee becomes the first out trans actor to be nominated for a Tony Award (*A Strange Loop*).

2023 Alex Newell and J. Harrison Ghee are the first out nonbinary actors to win Tony Awards (*Shucked, Some Like it Hot*).

Women of the Fur Trade by Frances Koncan premieres at the Stratford Festival (Ontario), directed by Yvette Nolan.

Index

Note: Page numbers followed by "n" denote endnotes.